SEMANTICS
AND EXPERIENCE

Parallax   Re-visions of Culture and Society

Stephen G. Nichols, Gerald Prince,
and Wendy Steiner, Series Editors

SEMANTICS AND EXPERIENCE

Universal Metaphors of Time in English, Mandarin, Hindi, and Sesotho

HOYT ALVERSON

The Johns Hopkins University Press

Baltimore and London

© 1994 The Johns Hopkins University Press
All rights reserved. Published 1994
Printed in the United States of America on acid-free paper
03 02 01 00 99 98 97 96 95 94   5 4 3 2 1

The Johns Hopkins University Press
2715 North Charles Street
Baltimore, Maryland 21218-4319
The Johns Hopkins Press Ltd., London

ISBN 0-8018-4811-3

Library of Congress Cataloging-in-Publication Data will be found at the end of
this book.

A catalog record for this book is available from the British Library.

With love to Marianne, Keith, and Brian,

who each wanted a different book,

none of them this one

CONTENTS

PREFACE

In the course of working with two languages, English and Setswana, during the three years I lived among the Tswana of southern Africa, I observed that between two languages verbs or nouns that designate what one might call mental states—intentions, abstract ideas, or feelings, including in particular the notions of time—could in general be translated quite exactly. Yet the two languages often exhibited great differences in the ways they each "mapped" words or phrases onto experiences of everyday visual scenes. I have noticed this also in translating from English to German, Mandarin, Hindi and other languages.

This raises an intriguing question: Why would unrelated languages, which until recently have had little contact, exhibit a great likeness or concordance of "experience-to-word-sense mapping" in those domains that are seemingly the most subjective—where experience seems to owe most to the mind's, or a particular culture's, unique contributions? Contrariwise, why would languages lexically encode so differently aspects of ordinary, physical space and objects arrayed in it, which would (or so one might think) perceptually induce a common objective experience on anyone beholding such scenes? These observations puzzled me all the more, since my research (and that of others working in eastern and southern Africa) has showed that at the level of overt ideas—ideology, philosophy, or folklore—the expression of what one might call temporal experience among eastern and southern African peoples certainly differs in significant ways from counterpart expressions in the modern West.

The topic and principal concern of this book is time—specifically, how one goes about asking and answering these questions: Are there universal as well as culturally particular experiences and expressions of time? What are they? How does one account for them? Study of these questions raises a fundamental issue—namely, how the meaning-bearing, meaning-expressing aspect of language enables people, despite the diversity and the linguistic, cultural, and geographic discontinuity of experience, to communicate and to believe that others grasp more or less precisely what one has said. Let me illustrate this point with an anecdote.

Some twenty-five years ago I was interviewing a South African man about his working experiences in a gold mine. I had asked him a question about events and developments that might take place in his life in the near future. In responding he said something seemingly paradoxical, which I subsequently heard, however, from many others: "It is impossible to know anything about the future; there can't be any future, because we have been severed from our origins." I asked my respondent to explain what that expression meant. The question must have showed me to be an ignoramus, for he said that its meaning was obvious and everyone knew it. Cajoling him—I was but a "child of Setswana" and he was my "uncle"—I received a very understandable answer that filled two pages.

Five years later I lived with my family in a small, rural agricultural community in southern Africa (Botswana) for two years, continuing the work I had carried out in the gold mine. Our life and residence there were on the community's terms, under its rules, and included intimate participation in the daily and seasonal round of life. Language, of course, served as the principal bridge between me—my background, needs, motives, and goals—and their world, with which I sought to become acquainted, to share, and to understand empathetically and as something to be explained.

My family and the village community met as strangers—inhabitants of places and a past unknown to either. We faced in very practical terms W.V.O. Quine's (1960) problem of "radical translation," but contrary to Quine's prediction, we learned much from our hosts and they from us, the sojourners. And when we bade farewell, I had come to understand much more fully that paradoxical expression I had first heard five years earlier.

This vignette exemplifies the important issue to which this

book seeks to make a contribution: how human language makes it possible to gain an understanding of a "world," which, in the instance cited, is as different from yours and mine as any two currently happen to be, and how language allows one to convey that understanding such that others, removed from all direct acquaintance with exotic experiences in that world, can come to share them. We will deal with this issue by examination of a very specific problem: the conditions of possibility for cross-language, cross-cultural translation of the experience and expression of time.

In the course of these several years' research in Africa, I came to the view that the human sciences have greatly exaggerated the ecological, institutional, and ideological differences among cultures of the world and hence the ways in which people experience their daily lives, including time. In my view, despite significant discontinuities and differences, the interlanguage and intercultural translation of experience (like that of time) is possible for two reasons: (1) we as humans share much fundamental experience in common to begin with, irrespective of cultural differences, and (2) the most important meaning-bearing aspects of all human languages gear into and express that experience in the same way.

The literature in anthropology and in other multi-cultural studies has, in the main, regarded the experience of time as a local cultural construction or hypostatization, and little more. The research reported here questions and challenges the cultural and conceptual relativism inherent in this majority view. This riposte consists of three interrelated tasks: (1) to motivate and describe a phenomenological approach to meaning as experience; (2) to describe two universal linguistic processes of categorization/typification—collocation and metaphor—which, along with the phenomenological account of meaning, provide a means of linking universals of grammatical (semantic) form with culturally universal and culturally contingent experience in linguistic expression; and (3) to illustrate by means of an indicative study in four languages and cultures that people everywhere experience and express time in fundamentally similar ways. I hope to show that the undeniable diversity in the experience and expression of time is situated in, and must be understood in terms of, a framework of experiential and linguistic universals.

Chapter 1 introduces the subject of time (temporality, duration) and illustrates my point that anthropology and other human sciences have overstated the variousness and diversity of temporal experience and, as a corollary, have little desire or means to explore and document temporal universals.

Chapter 2 describes an approach to (semantic) meaning in natural language (that based on work in cognitive grammar) which allows one to ground meaning in experiential universals and to investigate them in terms of linguistic expressions. Specifically, the perspective is introduced and justified which allows one to argue that the meaning of expressions in language is just human experience.

Chapter 3 introduces and advances the hypothesis—the spatialization of time—that the experience of time is based on a universal template of spatial experience. Methodological issues and procedures are described, which testing of the hypothesis entails.

Chapter 4 describes two universal linguistic processes in terms of which the study of time is cast: collocation and metaphor. I argue that these two linguistic processes express experience in all languages in the same way. Specifically, time is expressed in collocations—stock phrases, idioms, aphorisms, or other formulaic expressions—which gain their relative fixity from culturally patterned conditions of language use. These reflect, I argue, usage-induced attachments of words for one another and the ideological and institutional bases of communication. They arise from patterning in the use, acquisition, and transmission of language and the conditions of knowledge, situation, and purpose, of which language is always—at least tacitly—expressive. I hypothesize that experiential universals (including those of time) will be manifest in collocational and metaphoric universals. Because collocation is created in and reflects its context, it forms a kind of linguistic index of culture. Provided one can control for linguistic borrowing, collocations that appear and reappear in different languages, independent of cultural contingency, may reflect or express universal categories of experience.

In Chapter 5 a relational, metacultural definition of "time" is advanced, in terms of which I have gathered from native speakers of four languages—English, Mandarin, Hindi, and Sesotho—a corpus of collocations that are about or predicate properties of time. A categorization of these collocations for each language is made using as the criterion the kinds of metaphoric predications employed in the collocations. All of the data as classified are presented in Chapter 5.

In Chapter 6 I discuss the five basic metaphorically characterized universal categories of temporal expression and experience which appear in all four languages, despite the independence of these languages from one another and despite the very different conditions of belief, knowledge, and institutional structure which subsist among the cultures and communities that natively speak these respective languages. The collocations also reflect many culturally particular beliefs and practices. In these collocations we have direct discourse-engendered evidence of both universality and contingency in an important domain of experience—time—and evidence of how both are sedimented in linguistic expression.

In Chapter 7 I argue that these data and their analysis demonstrate the appositeness of a phenomenological or experiential approach to semantics—one developed in the book and illustrated in reference to the study of time. The chapter suggests some implications of these findings concerning time for the understanding of cognitive/experiential universals (possibly related to the prepredicative perception or apperception of space) and how, by means of language, these are appropriated as culturally particular experience.

I have tried to make this presentation accessible to scholars and students of those several disciplines that directly engage the study of meaning in natural language as well as those whose interests are in language use and culture. So, to breach the defenses of paradigmatic territory and reach as wide an audience as possible, I have made a number of compromises in style of writing and manner of argumentation. Specifically, I have sought to indicate the domain of validity of technical and formal arguments without encumbering the reader with a fully axiomatic account that some might reasonably demand. Conversely, I have not been satisfied simply to illustrate or instantiate formal arguments with linguistic anecdotes. The result is, I hope, a readable but rigorously demonstrated thesis, which those in linguistics, the behavioral and social sciences, literary theory, and philosophy might find important to their own work.

I want here to acknowledge the fine efforts of my linguistic and cultural "informants"—friends and colleagues who persisted in the often tedious work of uncovering relevant linguistic data and translating it, and in commenting on my linguistic and ethnographic analyses and conclusions: Hua-yuan Mowry, Li Kai, Umesh Madan, Krishen and Rekha Kak, Kiran Tankha, Subhobrata Joy Mitra, Seloka Phirwa, and Keitumetse Ruikers. Special thanks to Hua-yuan and Joy for their editorial help. Naturally, I am responsible for any errors and all interpretations and conclusions. John Watanabe kindly drew figure 1.

Hans Penner critically read early drafts of the manuscript, offering much sound advice and admonition. Steve Nichols did likewise and encouraged me to submit it to the Johns Hopkins University Press, where he eloquently argued for it during the review process.

A senior faculty research grant, a grant from the Claire Garber Goodman Fund for Anthropological Research, and a total of fifteen months sabbatical leave, all from Dartmouth College, provided the material support and time necessary to carry out both field research and writing. Thanks are due to Grace Buonocore, who meticulously copy-edited the typescript, as did Debbie Hodges, who also compiled the index.

SEMANTICS AND EXPERIENCE

CHAPTER ONE

On Time

For one to share something with others means (in a sense) to allow others to have or enjoy some of the "thing" in question. Now, if the thing to be shared is an experience, how does one share it? Well, to share it, one first must have it, and then one tells about it, usually in language. What one says or tells and what another understands is "sharing an experience." Though many beings, even machines, can communicate—that is, convey and analyze information—no beings except humans can have and then share any experience. Human language, of course, makes this possible.

To be able to share experiences—sometimes despite individual, geographic, cultural, or linguistic distinctness and difference—there must be common ways of having them to begin with and some relatively fixed way in which the meaning-bearing aspects of language gear into and express experience. That is, there must exist some universal experiential basis for what is called *meaning invariance* or *identity conditions on meaning,* which is constitutive of language itself. Translating among languages, sharing experiences with others, understanding other cultures all presuppose the existence of definite principles to which all languages, experiences, and cultures (and relationships among them) conform and therefore ways in which they are profoundly commensurate.

In much recent anthropology and other multicultural studies, a significant body of work has appeared which seems to ignore, contradict, or dispute the statement in the paragraph above. This literature exhibits a broad cultural, and even conceptual, relativism in its focus on linguistic, cultural, or historical particulars and differences. In one form, this school of thought sees each culture as a unique and particular expression of local history, ecology, institutions, and ideology. In another form, it seeks to define and partition claimed distinctness and difference in terms of larger spatial, temporal, or "developmental" groupings—for example, primitive versus civilized, traditional versus modern, cold versus hot, closed versus open, oriental versus occidental, Gemeinschaft versus Gesellschaft, preindustrial versus industrial, and so on. Keesing, in a critique of this trend, argues that

> the degree of cultural diversity in modes of thought and experience has been seriously and irresponsibly overstated in modern anthropology. . . . The powerful constraints inscribed on cultures by the biologically evolved brains and bodies of the creatures that learn and use them have been ignored and denied. Our spurious exoticizations have been sustained by . . . a refusal to attend to the evidence afforded by biology, cognitive sciences and linguistics. All this perpetuates a depiction of Otherness that hides our common humanness and its sources. (Keesing 1991:2)

Likewise, Gell, in a critical review of philosophic and anthropological scholarship on time, concludes:

> There is no fairyland where people experience time in a way that is markedly unlike the way in which we do ourselves, where there is no past, present and future, where time stands still, or chases its own tail, or swings back and forth like a pendulum. All of these possibilities have been seriously touted in the literature on the anthropology of time. . . . But they are all travesties engendered in the process of scholarly reflection. (Gell 1992:315)

Neither Keesing, Gell, nor I want to deny or ignore individual, cultural, historical, and ecological diversity. Rather, what is wanted, I (and they) argue, is to situate observed cultural/linguistic particulars within a theoretically defined framework of universals.

The subject of this text, and the topic I use to illustrate, expand upon, and respond to the points made above, is time—specifically, the culturally particular and culturally universal experiences and expressions of time as revealed in cosmogonies, in conventionalized reckoning, and, principally, in quotidian language use. This project aspires to deliver an account (paraphrasing Anna Wierzbicka, 1992) of the culturally specific configurations of a universal human concept, time.

There is a vast literature in anthropology and many other disciplines on the subject of time (see, in reference to anthropology, Nancy Munn's [1992:93–123] critical bibliographic essay, which covers 199 titles). This literature in the main manifests (Keesing and Gell obviously excepted) the highly relativistic view, which research reported here questions and challenges.

The relativist position asserts that temporal experience is constructed almost completely from indeterminately variable cultural particulars. How people experience time, it is argued, varies as a function of how the person's (or group's) language and culture hypostatize time. Because cultures (i.e., ecologies, institutions, ideologies, or languages) are in some sense very different across communities, experiences of time will be correlatively very different.

Undergirding this thesis, more or less explicitly, is the supposition that time's ontogeny (i.e., the character of its being) is indeterminate, either as a property of human beings or of the rest of the physical world. Time's supposed indeterminacy, like the indeterminacy of many things, gives local culture and language great scope to hypostatize it, largely according to local linguistic and cultural happenstance, tradition, exigency, or whatever. Most of this literature tacitly or directly denies an ontogeny of time, which (1) arises either from a panhuman (experiential) substratum or from properties of other physical phenomena, and which (2) necessarily affects or informs any and all linguistic or cultural hypostatizations. Let me document this claim simply by citing briefly four exemplary statements of this viewpoint (see Munn 1992 or Gell 1992 for a thorough bibliographic review).

Benjamin Lee Whorf (1940, 1956) provided a seminal modern linguistic and anthropological statement not only of conceptual, linguistic, and cultural relativity but also of its supposed manifestation in the experiences of time which characterize, respectively, the Hopi (a Pueblo people of the Southwest) and what he called "Standard Average European." Whorf says:

> Hopi may be called a timeless language. It recognizes psychological time, which is like Bergson's duration, but this "time" is quite unlike the mathematical time, T, used by our physicists. Among the peculiar properties of Hopi time are that it varies with each observer, does not permit of simultaneity, and has zero dimensions. . . . The timeless Hopi verb does not distinguish between present past and future of the event itself, but must always indicate what type of validity the speaker intends the statement to have. (Whorf 1940:247)

The larger thesis Whorf advanced (that of the linguistic relativity of experience in the tradition of von Humboldt) has since come to be known as the Sapir-Whorf hypothesis. All versions of this hypothesis postulate that there is some kind of correspondence between some aspect of the structure of a specific language and some aspect of experience. Stronger versions of the hypothesis argue that, because the correspondence is a result primarily of the relatively unchanging and unchangeable force of particular language properties, the structure of experiences remains stable and immune to change by ordinary variations in perception and cognition. The hypothesis argues further that differences in the structures of specific languages are causally related to differences in the structure of experience. The Sapir-Whorf hypothesis effectively blocks consideration of how the structure of human experience in general is affected by the faculty of language in general, precisely because the notion that languages are fundamentally alike was not and never has been a premise of the hypothesis. Indeed, its opposite has been—namely, that language structures differ markedly and incommensurately, and it is these differences that cause differences in experience (see Kay and Kempton 1983 for a detailed discussion).

Edmund Leach (1961), Clifford Geertz (1973c), and Edward Hall (1984) do not embrace the deterministic aspects of Whorf's linguistic relativism, but each asserts in one way or another that the experience of time is, at base, a linguistic/cultural hypostatization, which will be reflected in language use and especially in lexical categorizations. According to Leach:

Time . . . is a word which we use in a wide variety of contexts and it has a considerable number of synonyms, yet it is oddly difficult to translate. In an English-French dictionary time has one of the longest entries . . . ; time is *temps, foi, heur, âge, siècle* and *saison*. . . . The language of the Kachin people of North Burma seems to contain no single word which corresponds at all closely to English time. In the following expressions the Kachin equivalent of the word time would differ in every case.

The time by the clock is *ahkying*
A long time is *na*
A short time is *tawng*
The present time is *ten*
Spring time is *ta*
The time has come *hkra*
The time of Queen Victoria *lakhtak, aprat*
At any time of life *asak*

I do not think the Kachin would regard these as in any way synonyms for one another. This sort of thing suggests an interesting problem: how do we come to have such a verbal category as time at all? (Leach 1961:124–25)

Leach seems clearly to imply here that because the French and the Kachin have several words, the union of whose senses is contained in the set of senses of the single English word *time,* they therefore have an experiential category, time, which differs from ours. That is, a word's set of senses equals an experiential category.

There is an obvious problem with Leach's argument. In English we have distinct and different lexical morphemes for each of the Kachin notions illustrated, thus *ahkying* = hour, *na* = eon/age/epoch, *tawng* = moment/ second/twinkling/instant/flash, *ten* = present/currently, *ta* = spring, *hkra* = occasion, *lakhtak* = reign/era, *asak* = life stage/age. We do not conceive these as synonyms any more than the Kachin do. Do English speakers therefore have "views of time" which differ as a function of lexical choice? Hardly.

So what motivates Leach's conclusion that the Kachin have either a sense of time different from the French or from the English, or no sense of time at all? My assumption would be it is his presumption that distinct senses glossed by a single lexical morpheme create a different view or category of time than obtains when these same senses are glossed by several distinct and different words. This presumption is presumptuous. Further, the data Leach cites do not even show whether or not the Kachin have or don't have a counterpart for our word *time*. So the data beg the question, even if we concede his dubious presumption.

Geertz, in statements clearly intended to draw a stark contrast between conceptions and experiences of time in Bali and in the West, says:

> Balinese calendrical notions . . . are . . . used not to measure the elapse of time nor yet to accent the uniqueness and irrecoverability of the passing moment, but to mark and classify the qualitative modalities in terms of which time manifests itself in human experience. . . . The nature of time reckoning [of the calendric system] is not durational but punctual. That is, it is not used to measure the rate at which time passes, the amount which has passed since the occurrence of some event, or the amount of time which remains within which to complete some project: it is adapted and used for distinguishing and classifying discrete, self-subsistent particles of time. . . . They [the cycles of the calendar] don't tell you what time it is; they tell you what kind of time it is. (Geertz 1973c:391–93)

As we will see in chapters to come, there is probably in Geertz's formulation a conflation and maybe a confusion of the phenomenal particulars of the institutionally provided clock or calendric function with the way in which that clock function engenders experience.

Hall (1984) has popularized the thesis that, among the exotic and less civilized, time is filled with content, power, or purpose and is therefore very different from our Western one-dimensional, one-directional linear time, which is "woven into the fabric of life" as an aspect of everything yet which, on its own, is empty.

Demonstration of just how these exemplary "exoticizations" of time are misleading occupies the rest of this book, whose contrary, and perhaps contrarian, thesis is that the human experience called "time" (or alternatively, "temporality," "duration"), like most of human experience in general, is built upon and arises from a panhuman *Bauplan*. The research reported here shows, I believe, that all linguistic/cultural manifestations of temporal experience exhibit clearly the properties and effects of an underlying universal structure of embodied, enculturated mental experience.

This mental experience comports with none of the three most widely held views on the subject: (1) that of Kant, who averred that time does not originate in the senses but is presupposed by them—a subjective condition, owing to the nature of the human mind; (2) that of positivist science, which defines time as a variable of nature measured by clocks; or (3) that of relativistic anthropology, which sees time as a personification or construction of myth and ideology. What this panhuman experiential substratum does turn out to be is adduced by posing and answering two questions in terms of cross-language, cross-cultural inquiry: (1) What kind of experiences do ordinary linguistic expressions of time express? (2) How do they succeed in doing it? To properly investigate these questions requires, first, a carefully laid linguistic groundwork, to which we now turn.

CHAPTER TWO

Toward Phenomenological Semantics

I have asserted that there must be some way in which having experiences, sharing experiences, and expressing meaning in language are profoundly commensurate. This assertion says that "meaning" in human language must in some most fundamental way be *the expression in human language of human experience.*

"Meaning" so conceived builds upon work carried out over the past couple of decades as part of a research program in cognitive grammar. Ronald Langacker, a leader in developing and formulating cognitive grammar (1987, 1988, 1990), advances five theses concerning the nature of meaning in natural language (1988:49–50). Three of these are central to our investigation of "time": (1) meaning is mental experience; (2) semantic structures are characterized relative to cognitive domains; (3) semantic structures incorporate conventional imagery—that is, construe a situation in a particular fashion.

Our investigation of the experience and expression of time will illustrate and give substance to these three points, by (1) showing what and how a phenomenology of experience can contribute to linguistic semantics,[1] (2) providing an account of how necessarily

---

1. Phenomenology, the name for a congeries of philosophic schools and traditions in one way or another inspired by the work of the German mathematician-philosopher Edmund Husserl (1859–1939), began as a quest for the foundations of the meaning of logical and mathematical concepts and moved soon to an inquiry into the foundations of consciousness, knowing, and judgment, which are in turn supposed to provide the foundation of all science.

culture constitutes cognitive domains, and (3) demonstrating empirically that, while cognition is both culturally and linguistically schematized, there nevertheless may well be universal, pancultural experience incorporated in semantic structures and expressions of every language.

The conception of meaning in cognitive grammar is fundamentally phenomenological and differs from two very familiar approaches embraced singly or eclectically by most of contemporary linguistic semantics: *rationalist* and *empiricist* (see Fodor 1980; Newmeyer 1988). These approaches to semantics have presumed either a tabula rasa consciousness (e.g., the logical empiricism of Carnap 1966) or the irrelevance of particular experience (e.g., the rationalism of Katz 1972, 1979) for understanding meaning in language. In both cases language is seen as a system to be described apart from the species, and, in consequence, the character of experience and the relation of semantics to it have been ignored or defined in some very arbitrary and limited way. To wit, empiricism has delimited experience as sensory stimulation or observation and has limited semantic meaning to veridical representation, depiction, or description of sensorially transduced stimuli (coupled with a few "laws of thought"). Rationalism has sought to divorce meaning from particular experience and deal with it as an issue of logical form and coherence.

All this has unnecessarily and unproductively forced onto semantics a dichotomy-plagued theoretical language: competence-performance, meaning-force, ideal-real, semantic-pragmatic, lexical-encyclopedic, sense-reference, definitional-associated concepts, intuitive-interpretive, literal-figurative, and so on. I argue that these contrivances are made necessary by the dubious supposition that certain uses, regimentations, or possible capacities of language are uniquely its canonic form.

A phenomenological semantics restores experience to meaning, which requires that language be studied as an organic part of our species. As one philosopher of science puts it, "reflections on the limitations of human nature—perhaps reinforced by considerations of the extent to which the capacities of the human senses and intelligence are conditioned by our biological peculiarity may convince us that there are certain *vantage points* t are forever tied by our humanity and hence cannot hope to transcend in our scientific theories" (Jardine 1980:23; emphasis added).

From this it surely follows, contra empiricism, that the notion of representing in language the world as it actually is must be incoherent, for "we could have no conception of the world that transcends all possible ways of representing it. Though the world may be prised away from our manner of conceiving it, it cannot be prised away from every possible manner of conceiving it" (Jardine 1980:24). Therefore, by implication, the so-called actual world (physical reality) could not by itself be the basis for universals of human experience. In relation to our topic, time (and the tandem issue of space, with which we also must deal), the physicist Henry Margenau sounds a phenomenological caveat for empiricists:

> One must carefully guard against the temptation to hypostatize space into an entity given in and through immediate sensation, pervading all experience, and with its properties fixed eternally by observation. Space is not wholly an abstraction . . . from direct perception. . . . We hold it to be a construct. . . . Indeed, nowhere does the constructional character of physical concepts become more manifest than in the analysis of space and time. . . . Unlike many physical quantities, space and time cannot be directly perceived. In this they differ from mass and force. . . . For there is something in the [perceptual] field called mass (the awareness of something impenetrable), there is something called force (sensation of muscular exertion). . . . Time and space seem to lack that tangible quality in the perceptual field and to present themselves under these names primarily as constructs. . . . The words space and time rarely have reference exclusively to Nature. (Margenau 1950:128–29)

Margenau is referring here to the prereflective experience of crude space, not to a philosophy for physics. If Margenau's statement is correct—and I believe it is—then the view that the experience of space (or time) can be reduced to sensory perception or to a sense datum must be substantially in error.

In the recent past, the regimentations of language required by the ideology of positivistic science have served as a canonic form of language for purposes of much linguistic—especially semantic—analysis. Positivism's *prescriptive* model of the proper nature and use of formal language—that is, that there should be, in Ryle's words, some "real, non-conventional one-to-one relationship between the composition of the expression and the composition of the fact" (Mohanty 1970:69)—has been adopted as a *descriptive* model of meaning in linguistic semantics. In this view, meaning in language is understood in terms of either the veridical description of some putative bottom-line reality or the transcendent rationality of logical forms.

A resolution or reconciliation of rationalist and empiricist insights requires a rethinking and recasting of the problem of meaning invariance in natural language. Meaning invariance, the semantic-pragmatic linkage (how language gears into the world), and the acquisition of the meaning component of language require, I argue, a semantics based on a phenomenology of human experience.

Such a phenomenological semantics is a theory of meaning based and focused on the nature of human experience, which is tied up completely with the character of human capabilities—perceptual, cognitive, cultural. In Johnson's words, "a theory of meaning is a theory of how we understand things . . . how an individual as embedded in a linguistic community, a culture, and a historical context understands" (1987:190).

For phenomenological semantics, perception, cognition, and behavior in animal species have to be the consequence of an evolutionary process. Whatever phenotypic characteristics (behavioral or morphologic) a species exhibits, they are assumed to be, in some degree, a result of genetic and environmental interactions favored by natural selection. Thus the parameters of a species' cognizing of, and behavior in, its "world" must be a product in some measure of genetically engendered phenotypic variation and consequent selective—that is, reproductive—advantage.

All this applies to our species, *Homo sapiens*, and bears directly on the issue of what human experience (including that of our topic, time) is seen to be. Human capabilities of perception, cognition, language, and culture are each forces of selection in and products of organic evolution. To a degree that we cannot now ascertain or measure, we experience what we do in the way we do simply because the organic substratum of that experience has been successful—that is, it has conferred some reproductive advantage.

It would be utterly fantastic if human language were *not* a product evolving in concert with the rest of the human phenotype, including its perceptual, cognitive, and motivational components. Language, a species-specific endowment of *Homo sapiens*, probably appeared and evolved with our genus, *Homo*. Therefore, the character of language, including its semantics, must be understood in terms of the species that possesses it. Language, to be a selective force and selective product of evolution, had to be expressed overtly—in speaking and communicating. But that overt expression of language upon which selection operated could not have been confined to the level of determinate vocalization or specific messages. Had this been so, specific languages, even specific utterances, would have become genotypically "wired in."

What seems to have been "wired in" instead is the capability for language, which entails the capability for acquiring nondenumerably many specific languages. For this to have occurred, each and every language must have expressed the same underlying capability in order for natural selection to have operated in the same fashion, with the same consequences, on each language spoken by communities of our species in the genus *Homo*. Further, the genetic changes making language possible were most likely based or overlaid upon universal, invariant, antecedent genetic/phenotypic traits (see Lightfoot 1987 or Bickerton 1990 for a full account of the perspective stated here).

Insofar as "universal grammar" correctly describes the underlying capability for language, it constitutes a model of language's organic substratum. Although considerable progress has been made in the last thirty years in describing the phonologic and syntactic components of universal grammar, progress on the semantic component has been quite limited, primarily, I argue, because the ontologic commitments of rationalism and empiricism have led us to start with misleading assumptions and the wrong questions concerning what language is about: human experience.

Phenomenology's conception of experience opposes that of rationalism and of empiricism in that it includes the so-called vantage point as an ineluctable—indeed, essential—aspect of experience. Experience for humans is necessarily *intentional*—"for us," "in a certain manner," "from a certain standpoint," "as conceived, known, or described," which implies a mode of knowing or of apprehension. Colin McGinn (1981:165) says that modal knowing presumes a cognitive faculty that postulates: (1) a factive world, (2) a mode of knowing it, (3) a gap between them, and (4) no possibility for reduction (because of the impossibility of absolutism) of these three to a direct apprehension and knowledge of the actual world. "Modal knowing" means that any thing, as experienced, will be a function of each mode of (cognitive) presentation—that is, each way a thing is intended (for a full discussion see Edie 1987 or Ricoeur 1967).

This formulation in no way denies—indeed, it acknowledges—the existence of a brute, actual reality independent of human capacities, purposes, or awareness. What it does deny is that experience, including belief or knowledge, could consist in direct or immediate apprehension of such a reality and, by extension, that semantics could have anything to do with such an unknowable, transcendently actual realm. Likewise, it rejects as spurious Descartes's thought experiment, which purported to demonstrate that there is a pure *cogito*—thought and thinking minus the thinker and his or her world. Descartes's *cogito* never abandoned its *ego*—that is, its culture, cognitive processes, and common sense—even in its most abstract reflections. This is nowhere clearer than in his thinking about thought on analogy with how science of that period thought about visual perception.

Now, one must ask what makes human experience, so conceived, a firmer foundation for semantic meaning than that provided by human acts or purposes, as argued by functionalists. After all, acts and purposes are kinds of human experience. Yet the semantic component of language cannot be simply an encoding of each individual's subjective stock of acts, purposes, thoughts, and other experiences, lest every attempted linguistic communication become a project in radical translation between two speakers, each using a private language. Such a conception of the semantic component is no better, and may be worse, than what rationalists and empiricists have already offered.

An adequate response to this well-motivated objection has, in my view, two parts. First, semantics can be based on experience, as defined, only if we discover a pancultural and panlinguistic dimension of experience upon which to build a theory of meaning. Human acts and purposes presuppose particular languages in particular cultures. This is not true, I argue, for all human experience, dimensions or aspects of which are pancultural or panlinguistic or both. As James Edie puts it, "language is intrinsically apresentational of experience and therefore is anthropocentric. . . . We invest objects of thought with the familiar—prepredicative, pre-reflective, pre-theoretical aspects of the lived body experience" (1976:161).

Second, there must be linguistically universal processes whereby previous, and possibly basal, experience is expanded and stored in principled, but not determinate, fashion in discourse and thence in the lexicon—what Giambattista Vico describes as the "power of the mind to think by means of its more primary experience of perception" (quoted in Edie 1976:168).

This issue of a panhuman experiential basis for meaning invariance poses a vexing problem: there is a necessary conflation of that which is locally, historically, and culturally acquired and linguistically sedimented with that which is a priori endogenous to language as such (and therefore all languages), irrespective of cultural contingency. Given this conflation, how is one to discern in language those aspects or moments of the meaning/experience "time" which are traceable to specific cultural/historical contexts versus those that arise because of some supposed panhuman experiential substratum?

Let me reframe the problem assertively. To say there is a necessary conflation of the universal and the particular in the background of human experience is to say that human nature does not and cannot subsist in distinct ontologic strata, where the lower strata are deemed to have arisen prior to, and to be

unaffected by, the latter. Clifford Geertz (1973a, 1973b) has eloquently described the problem of viewing human experience as if
it exists in distinct strata. This view misleads us into thinking that
if we peel away individuality, we get culture; if we peel away
culture, we get psyche; if we peel away psyche, we get the organic
meat machine; if we peel that away, we get cells, then chemical,
atomic, and subatomic interactions. Geertz notes that if we peel
away culture, we don't get basic human psychological nature; we
get a monstrosity—and a purely fictional one at that.

This lack of stratification poses a serious problem for any
cognitive or phenomenological semantics that seeks to discover
universal bases for human experience. A given regularity, uniformity, or universality in experience or its linguistic expression may
or may not indicate that such a form is somehow prior to culture,
because there are many universals of human experience not
traceable uniquely to pristinely conceived linguistic, psychological, or biological processes. After all, we live in a material world,
important universals of which exist in virtue of the whole of
"nature," including culturally organized productive processes.
Every speaker, every speech community is part of a pregiven
material world that comprises a skein of cultural-historical production that manifests both universal and specific components.
Meanings in language simply cannot constitute or express a
perceptual yet culturally unmediated experience of the world,
precisely because nobody has, ever has had, or ever could have
such an experience. However, the fact that there is no culturally
unmediated experience does not imply that there are no universals of experience—that is, "embodied experience." In our comparative study of time through language form, I try to show how
one can untangle this conflation of the universal and the particular.

CATEGORIZATION AND MODALITY

Our discussion of phenomenology invites us to understand the
question "What is time" as a question about language and
language use. Specifically, the question "What is time" means,

phenomenologically, how the category time is constituted and expressed in human language. Now, categorization, I have asserted, entails modality in knowing, thinking, or experiencing. Categorization, in whatever form, "tells" a person how experience engenders significance. Hence our questions about time are in effect questions about the modal, categorial character of human experience.

Categorial experience is seeing the world not in terms of brute sensation but in terms of the messages the brute things (whatever they might be) signify for us. So, for example, acts of seeing are acts of "seeing things signify." When one *says* "I see (an) X," what one is *doing* is judging X to signify a category, type, paragon, or schema coded in the language. X's meaning is its categorization, which in human language entails modality.

While it may seem like a digression, we cannot go directly to a study of time without first establishing a clear understanding of how categorization and modality generally affect and inform all human experience. This discussion will also help clarify key phenomenological concepts cursorily introduced above.

"A theory of categorization is basic to any theory of cognitive structure, for it explores the way we organize our experience into *kinds.* We need an analysis of the levels of categories, with special emphasis on those that are 'basic level,' the level of organization that is experientially predominant for a given organism. This level will be determined by the way people interact with their environment. . . . In short, categorization will be understood within a general theory of cognitive models" (Johnson 1987:191–92).

Jackendoff is in full accord: "[T]he principles for TYPE [i.e., category] formation and for TYPE assignment are generally unconscious, as are the principles described above for projecting 'individual entities.' No question has vexed the human sciences more than 'what are the principles encoded in a TYPE like?'" (Jackendoff 1983:84). "In general, the rules encoded in a TYPE are not available to consciousness; they cannot be taught. . . . A good proportion of [TYPE] teaching [*sic*!] is necessarily limited to the presentation of examples, leaving the student to figure out the principles. . . . *I am inclined to consider the theory of this process to be about the most fundamental problem of cognitive psychology"* (Jackendoff 1983:86–87; emphasis added).

Phenomenologically, the categorization process consists in two elements: (1) the presence of a cognitive model of some sort (schema, paragon, prototype, set of features, function, etc.) which (2) one judges a given experience to belong to, satisfy, instantiate, or exemplify. Categorization, then, entails or presupposes judgment. As we will see presently, categorization or typification serves to link the sensory with signification. Whatever the inherent properties or qualities of a percept X, including its brute existence or lack of it, their importance in perception or other experience is not their actuality or givenness but how it is that the perceiver justifies, by means of these qualities or properties, the judgment that perception of X is perception of an instance of a given category, type, class, or paragon. The thing-as-experienced is a signifier, that is—it signifies its category.

Let us be clear at the outset on what this last proposition necessarily precludes, for there is some confusion in the literature on this (see, for example, Jackendoff 1983:51, *passim*; Bickerton 1990:105–63). Because categorization entails judgment, it cannot be an instance of, equated to, or reduced to "stimulus generalization," as exhibited in the responses of animals to operant conditioning.

While stimulus and response generalization in animal-conditioning experiments may be formally (albeit anthropomorphically) represented as though they were judgments, in fact these are entirely different phenomena, for one presupposes language and culturally organized belief and knowledge that the other does not. Stimulus generalization happens the way light dilates the pupil of the eye or a loud noise causes one to wince. It is involuntary behavior.

Among infrahuman animals, we infer that two stimuli are for the animal "the same" or "similar" insofar as their presence to the animal is associated with the same responses, physiologic or behavioral. In the cant of behaviorism, if one "conditions" an animal to respond with some specific behavior to a stimulus, X, then insofar as X1, X2, X3, and so on elicit the same response, the animal's behavior is deemed to evidence "stimulus generalization." The phenomenally various Xs become functionally, for the animal, the same (stimulus). Sameness (or similarity) of stimulus condition is operationally determined by response sameness or similarity—all, of course, as judged by the observing, human experimenter.

In the case of humans, we cannot infer whether two stimuli are identical, the same, similar, different, or incommensurate by describing from some God's-eye view perceptual properties or by observing (response) behavior. Stimulus properties, so called, are relevant to human behavior in ways very different from what obtains among nonhuman animals, precisely because properties (all properties), as we have seen, are properties as they may signify.

To categorize is to judge; therefore judging, unlike stimulus generalization, constitutes a motivated relationship of a particular kind between a consciousness and an object of consciousness. It implicates an attitude or standpoint, as well as an object of experience.

The simple statement "TOKEN$_i$ is an instance of TYPE$_j$," or "TYPE$_j$ typifies TOKEN$_i$," fails to disclose the necessarily modal or cognitively perspectival part of the experience. Despite the seemingly transparent character of these statements, categorization is not an open window onto experience; rather, it is always necessarily the expression of experience in an opaque context—the *how* as well as the *what*.

Jackendoff notes an important implication of this intentional, cognitively perspectival character of categorization: he takes issue with "the naive and nearly universally accepted . . . [view] that information conveyed [in/by language] is about the real world" (1983:29), if only because "vast areas of our experience are due to the mind's contribution" that "we are normally unaware of" (1983:26–27). He insists that "environmental inputs" be distinguished from what is experienced—what he calls the "projected world." "Information conveyed by language must be about the projected world, . . . [and therefore] we must question the centrality to natural language of the notions truth and reference as traditionally conceived" (1983:29). "These [e.g., entity, thing, place, state, property, direction, action, event, manner, amount] are not reducible to states of affairs in some real world but are primitives of conceptual structure itself" (1983:51). "Thinghood," for example, could not be given to perception by the "real" world, for "THING cannot be straightforwardly correlated with reality. . . . The literature on perception is concerned with how we manage the remarkable feat of construing the #world# as full of more or less stable #things#, given constantly shifting patterns of environmental stimulation" (1983:51). Under this approach, linguistic semantics is not concerned with

> reducing out events, places, and so forth from the formal description, but with clarifying their psychological nature and showing how they are expressed syntactically and lexically. . . . The existence of a particular ontologic category is not a matter of physics, metaphysical speculation, or formal parsimony, but an empirical psychological issue to be determined on the basis of its value in explaining the experience and behavior of humans and other organisms, [and] the total set of ontologic categories must be universal: it constitutes one basic dimension along which humans can organize their experience, and hence it cannot be learned. (Jackendoff 1983:51–52, 56)

Likewise, Lakoff argues that the only thing language can be about is experience, the base of which he claims is prepredicative. To wit,

> meaningfulness derives from the experience of functioning as a being of a certain sort in an environment of a certain sort. Basic level concepts are meaningful to us because they are characterized by the way we perceive the overall shape of things . . . and by the way we interact with things with our bodies. Image schemas are meaningful to us because of the way they structure our perception. . . . Metaphors are meaningful because they are based on directly meaningful concepts and correlations in our experience. (Lakoff 1987:292)

This is contrary to the Aristotelian notion that categories express necessary and sufficient conditions for membership which are satisfied by assemblages of objective properties inhering in phenomena. Of course the meanings of some words can be related or described in terms of "necessary conditions"[2]—for example, red entails color, game entails human play, uncle entails male—and in general, words of various lexical categories map into basic ontologic categories—for example, event, thing, property, manner, place, direction, amount—making them also necessary conditions on word meaning.

Word meanings often comprise "typicality conditions." These are the specific values, characteristics, or qualities that experienced objects modally possess. These ideal-typic features will usually be type specific (the typical red of apples is not the same color as the typical red of house paint) and do not constitute a definite set. Numbers of the typifying attributes may be absent or manifest atypical values without changing the type designation—for example, a three-legged dog, a flightless bird. (Obviously, such a view of meaning immediately implicates cultural norms.)

The approach to the study of categorization by means of prototypification, family resemblances, scenarios, and schematization is large and growing. A summation is impossible here (see, for example, Berlin 1968; Berlin, Breedlove, and Raven 1974; Berlin and Kay 1969; Kay 1979; Kay and McDaniel 1978; Kempton 1981; Rosch 1973, 1975, 1977, 1978, 1981; and Rudzka-Ostyn 1988). The literature on categorization by tropes (especially metaphor) is vast (see Fernandez 1991; Lakoff 1987; and Lakoff and Johnson 1980).

---

2. This approach to semantics is represented in the work of anthropologists who have applied principles of Prague School phonology to the study or construction of "semantic fields" (for important examples of this work, see Lévi-Strauss 1966; Tyler 1987). In this enterprise, certain highly structured or devised classification systems—kinship systems, nosologies, topographic nomenclatures, plant and animal taxonomies, culinary procedures, and the like—could be described by combinatorial or other syntactically simple use of underlying semantic features or markers. These underlying components of meaning give the necessary and sufficient conditions, satisfaction of which makes a phenomenon a designation of a sense of a term in the vocabulary in question. Anthropologists have hotly debated the psychological or cognitive reality, as well as the formal adequacy, of these "componential analyses" of systems of nomenclature (see Alverson 1984 for a linguistic critique and Tyler 1978:186–210 for a cultural one).

What physicists call the "constructional" dimension of reality some linguists, anthropologists, and psychologists have described cognately as the "schematization" of experience. A substantial literature deals with cognition and other experience in terms of schemata, especially those of linguistic origin (see Abelson and Schank 1977; Casson 1981; Graesser and Clark 1985; Holland 1987; Kempton 1981; and Tyler 1978, 1987a). Because our study of time requires dealing with categorization by means of such schematization in language, I want to discuss a few concrete examples to clarify what this literature tells us.

The sentence "I saw John *wave*" categorizes an experience: I saw an intentional object "waving," as opposed to the behaviorally identical but differently intended object "moving the open hand up and down." "I saw John *wink*" reports or expresses seeing an intentional object different from the behaviorally identical one "blink." "I saw the pitcher walk three men in a row" reports my seeing in terms of the intention created by knowing the rules of baseball. Ptolemy, in seeing "the sun," saw a *planet*. Copernicus, in seeing "the sun," saw a *star*. The two different intentional objects were created by the two different theories held. Take another kind of "seeing":

$$x = \frac{-b \pm \sqrt{b^2 - 4ac}}{2a}$$

Someone unfamiliar with algebra "sees" a collection of marks that perhaps signify the alphabetic and numeric; a mathematician immediately "sees" the quadratic formula. Seeing a glass half full "intends" the glass's contents differently than does seeing "the glass half empty." This phenomenological point can be illustrated by means of a simple visual experience.

Consider the scene below. In it I depict by means of conventional markings a person (viewer) gazing at what for him or her is "straight ahead." (For you, this is from lower left to upper right diagonally across the page.) Directly in the path of the gaze and receding from you and the viewer are first a pumpkin, second a tree, and third a box. Anyone in the position of the viewer who wishes to describe that scene has to do it *modally*. That is, any

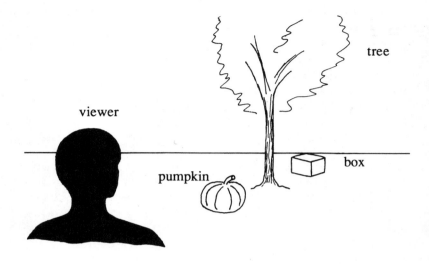

Figure 1

description will be a selective expression of cognitive/perceptual, cultural information, which both underdetermines the scene (says less than one might "see") and overinterprets it (bestows on it interpretations not given in the drawing).

An interesting illustration of how such modality can be built into language is found in the contrast between the way a speaker of a Germanic or Romance language and a speaker of all Bantu languages I know of would describe the spatial relationships of the objects when one takes the perspective of the viewer. "We," were we the viewer, would say: (1) the pumpkin is in front of me, (2) the pumpkin is in front of the tree, (3) the box is behind the tree, (4) the tree is in front of me, and, possibly, (5) I am in front of the tree.

A speaker of a Bantu language would say of this same configuration, were she or he the viewer: (1) the pumpkin is in front of me, (2) the tree is in front of the pumpkin, (3) the box is in front of the tree, (4) the tree is behind the box, (5) the pumpkin is behind the tree, and (6) I am behind the pumpkin. The dimension of modality distinguishing the two sets of descriptions is that for "us" the primary anchorage for spatial relations in this visual field is *relative object size*: larger objects coordinate the location of smaller objects. (If any of the objects had had a face or orientation, then that might take precedence over size.) For the Bantu speaker, the direction of the gaze serves as the primary anchorage or coordination of spatial relations in this scene irrespective of object size. Thus "ahead" is always in front of; "less far ahead" is behind.

That descriptions are always modally related to what is described is a restatement of the notion that what sentences express is always modally related to what they might pragmatically refer to. This view contradicts the empiricist stance, which argues that there can be a "neutral" or "objective" description of a scene (see, for example, Barwise and Perry 1983). Any description of a scene necessarily describes how it is seen. There are no theoretically or intentionally "neutral" descriptions of any percept, for all perception depends in part on inferences not given in the percept.

Take, for example, the kind of categorization of a spatial scene or array expressed in English by various senses of the word *over* (see Alverson 1991 for a fuller discussion of this example). The collected senses of *over* in contemporary American English would appear to express various partitionings of the experience of viewing from below a point that radiates out and covers a surface and is in motion such as to describe an arclike course. A real-world counterpart of this is viewing the sun in its dial. Here we have an intentional scene in which the point can be seen as in motion or still (depending on intention). The movement of the object describes a trajectory. The object is either a point (of light) or a sweeping effect, making contact with and covering the surface (rays of the sun). The gaze on this scene takes place from below the point (of light). The trajectory goes over or across terrain. At any instant, the point of light describes a point above a surface in a vertical axis. The sun makes contact with the surface via sunlight, but the sun itself is always above and not in contact with the terrain. The dial (movement) of the sun is repetitive— that is, it creates the recurrence of identical events. At the horizon, the trajectory appears to transect the surface. The view in imagination can occupy any point in the scene.

It would seem that aspectually or perspectivally beholding this scene can generate all the various categorial properties expressed in the senses of the word *over*. Consider the list in table 1.

Words used in the three languages which express the respective "over" experiences:

English: over
German: *vorbei* + *hinweg*, *über* (+ dative + accusative),
hinter (+ dative), *an*, and *um*,
Setswana: *kwa*, *kwa godimo ga*, *godimo ga*, *kakwa godimo*, *mo*,
mo godimo ga, *ka kwa ga*, *kwa* + *-eng*, *kakwa* + *-eng*,
mo + *-eng*, *ka*, and unmarked morphologically

Since this scene is a rich and full one, there may be many extensions of the scene that no typified, extant sense of *over* quite captures. For example, *overtake* used to mean pursuing with the intent of pouncing upon or coming down on from above (as with prey). Does not the sun do this at the horizon as it "chases the night"? The sun is of course powerful—its rays can burn—and its power is greatest when directly over (she has power over me?). What more clearly than the sun is an entity that does and does not make contact with landmarks on the surface? What more clearly than the sun goes above, goes across, stands still, travels great distances, describes a trajectory, covers, reflexively moves around a central axis? (The sun goes over each day, over and over and over.) It fills the world with energy and plenty, yet too much of it (excess) can damage. Day is over when the sun sets. The sun (moon, stars) fall (over) the horizon. At daybreak the light floods, overflows the land. The sun conquers darkness (overthrows it).

The scene I have described can potentially motivate all the experiences required to schematize every sense that the word *over* has, has had, or probably ever will have. It may also motivate experiences glossed by senses of other prepositions and their metaphoric extensions as well, as we see indubitably in the case of Setswana and German. The words *über* and *ka*, however, partition this scene differently. They represent a different assem-

Table 1

English	German	Setswana
1. The bird flew *over*/(past).	Der Vogel ist *vorbei*geflogen.	Nonyane e fofile *kwa godimo*.
2. The bird flew (that way) *over* the field.	Der Vogel ist *über* das Feld hinweg geflogen.	Nonyane e fofile *go dimo ga* masimo.
3. The bird flew *over* the mountain.	Der Vogel verschwand *hinter* dem Hugel.	Nonyane e fofile *ka kwa ga* thaba.
4. The balloon is (floating) *over* the garden.	Der Ballon ist *über* dem Garten.	Leballon le dutse mo moweng o *mo godimo ga* lolwapa.
5. Sam walked *over* the hill.	Sam ging *über* den Hügel.	Sam oile *ka kwa ga* thaba.
6. Sam lives *over* the hill.	Sam wohnt *hinter* dem Berg.	Sam oagile *ka kwa ga* thaba.
7. The pot is hanging *over* the fire	Der Topf hängt *über* dem Feuer.	Pitse e elekeletse *godimo ga* molelo.
8. Sam jumped *over* the wall.	Sam sprang *über* die Mauer.	Sam oile otlota leraka.
9. The plank is *over* the hole.	Das Brett ist *über* dem Loch.	Leplanka le *godimo ga* mokote.
10. Police were posted *(all) over* the hill.	Polizisten wurden *über* den ganzen Hugel verteilt.	Go ne go tletse mapodise *mo godimo ga* thaba.
11. Sam has gone *over* to the hill.	Sam ist zu dem Hügel *hinüber* gegangen.	Sam oile *ka kwa* thabeng.
12. Sam walked all *over* the hill.	Sam ist *über* den ganzen Hügel gewandert.	Sam otsamaile a tsamaya fela *mo* thabeng.
13. Sam has a veil *over* his face.	Sam hat einen Schleier *über* seinem Gesicht.	Sam okwetse sefatlhogo *ka* lesere.
14. Sam climbed *over* the canyon walls.	Sam kletterte *an/(in)* den Kanyonwänden.	Sam opalame *kwa ga* logago.
15. Sam rolled the log *over*.	Sam rollte den Baum *um*.	Sam odikolositse morapatse.
16. Sam turned the leaf *over*.	Sam drehte das Blatt *um*.	Sam oemisitse letlhare.
17. The fence fell *over*.	Der Zaun ist *um*gefallen.	Leraka lewile.

Table 1, *continued*

English	German	Setswana
18. Sam knocked *over* the lamp.	Sam hat die Lampe *um*gestossen.	Sam owisitse lesedi.
19. The water (in the river) *over*flowed.	Das Wasser im Fluss ist *über*geflossen.	Noka etletse go tlala.
20. Sam asked him to come *over*.	Sam bat ihn *herüber*zukommen.	Sam omolaleditse go tla *ka kwano*.

blage of gazes or perspectives. Some of the particular gazes that they represent can also be represented by *over*; others cannot. To prefigure an issue we take up below concerning time, what these data from the three languages do *not* allow us to conclude is that the English, German, and Setswana have different categories of "over"-type experiences, just because the distribution of (semantic) senses is mapped onto one word or phrase in English, five in German, and fourteen in Setswana. Recall that this is what Leach tried to claim in his observations on time in English, French, and Kachin.

Categorization or schematization of a scene, however it is lexically or phrasally encoded, renders it necessarily an intentional object. There is systematic selection, abstraction, idealization, and—most important—bestowal of qualities or properties to the experience of referential scenes.

Talmy (1983:1–33) describes several features of spatial schemata found in language. Our description of the "over" schema exemplifies all of them. First, there is a *figure-ground contrast*—something coordinates the space, while other things are located within the coordinates. Second, there is a *biased topology* of objects and the array. The objects and array will have asymmetric parts (front-back, up-down, right-left, directionality) and normative orientation (e.g., upright, overturned). Third, the objects and array will exhibit topologic *relationships of attitude and proximity.* Fourth, there will be a hypothetical *perspective point* on the scene—that is, the schemata depict the scenes as seen. Fifth, the *distribution of mental attention* to the scene from the perspective point will be indicated. Sixth, there will be a *force dynamics* imputed to the scene: What is making the scene appear this way? What is happening, tends to happen, or might happen? Seventh, there will be *idealization* of the scene—that is, schemata are never actual scenes in their "bulk and physicality."

In the words of mathematician Hermann Weyl: "Within the concrete unity of perception, the data of sensation are animated by interpretations and only in unison with them do they perform the function of representation and help to constitute what we call the appearance of . . . [something]" (1970:96). In consequence, an individual (or perhaps a culture) may "choose" to schematize a perceived scene in indefinitely many ways, many mutually contradictory. Because of the interpretive/intentional character of perception, a scene always underdetermines its schematization, and a schematization always overinterprets or overflows its putative referent.

These points concerning the intentional topology of scenes are sometimes missed. For example, George Lakoff (1987:425) says that the "above" sense of *over* precludes "contact" and "path." This is exemplified by a sentence like "the picture is over the fireplace." However, the notion of "path" as a constituent of the sense of the word *over* is not Euclidean. Thus we can say "the ribbon is draped over the car" (where there is contact) but not "the ribbon is over the car" (which would imply that the ribbon is somehow suspended). The resolution of this apparent paradox is simple: the notions of "covering" and the notions of "path" have to be construed intentionally rather than actualistically. Thus a ribbon can be construed as describing a path, provided it is laid out. And it can be construed as covering, and hence requiring contact, provided it is draped.

In another case, Lakoff says, "end point focus [a horizontal here-to-there orientation] can only be added . . . to those schemas . . . with extended [here-to-there] landmarks" (1987:422). This is true intentionally but not actualistically, because extension is intentional (no oxymoronic pun intended). Thus, according to Lakoff, a wall, as in "Sam jumped over the wall," is not a (horizontally) extended landmark. So if we say, "Sam lives over the wall," we imply a house suspended over the wall. The wall lacks "end point focus," says Lakoff, because it is not extended.

But a wall can be extended intentionally. Thus I can say "Where's the chipmunk's hole?" "It's just over the wall," clearly implying end point focus as is found in sentences like "Sam lives over the hill/bridge/mountain." In the case of the wall, the gaze of the speaker or addressee constructs the scene so as to intend a path to the other side of the wall and hence the possibility of an end point.

In another place Lakoff asserts that the "above" sense of *over* "is roughly equivalent in meaning to 'above'" (1987:419). This flows from a sense of categorization by image schema which ignores intentional geometry. *Over* in this sense has an intentional horizon that "above" *simpliciter* does not have. While typically precluding contact, *over* in this sense retains the sense of intimacy of intentional connection or relation between the landmark and the object and the sense of trajectory that covers or crosses (just as the sun does not touch but is in connection with the earth and its orbit covers/crosses the sky). A roof is not "above" but "over" the house. A fly is not over the fireplace because the intimate connection between "fly" and "fireplace" is not intended by the wall, which creates such a connection when a picture is hung over the fireplace (on the wall). *Over* in this sense signifies a relationship between reference landmark and object. We can't say "on the shelf just over" (compare "above"). We can't say "the guest suite is one flight 'over'" (meaning "above") because there is no relation to the below.

Over does not easily let go of its sense of arclike trajectory. A given skyscraper may rise above but not over the city, but that same building may be intended differently, as when it towers over but not above the city. Hills may overlook the city or be above the city, and a hut on those hills may overlook the city, but the hut is not over the city, even if it is both above it and overlooks it! This makes sense only if we conceive scenes as categorized to be intentional, conventional (i.e., culturally informed) significance-bestowing devices, not as actualistic depictions of geometric configurations.[3]

---

3. These phenomenological points are true of experiences of any sort, including those expressed in the most abstract propositions or concepts. For example, in

THE INTENTIONAL, CATEGORIAL NATURE OF
SEMANTIC "INDIVIDUALS"

What has just been said about "categories" or "types" can be extended *pari passu* to "individuals." So we may ask, where do "individuals" (also called "tokens") which refer to, represent, or express in language a world of #individuals# come from?

It might seem plausible to explain by reference to untutored, nonintentional perception our belief that the "sun" is simply

---

logic it is customary to think of logical sentences as having three kinds of constituents: arguments or terms (constant and variable), quantifiers, and predicates. Predicates are thought of as specifying a property of one or more arguments. In a sentence like "Hoyt remembered p," where "p" is any proposition like "he gave the speech," "his giving the speech," "giving the speech," "himself giving the speech," and so on, the predicate "remembered" is said to predicate a property of—for example—a relationship between a pair of terms or arguments, (1) Hoyt (the subject) and (2) Hoyt gave the speech (the predicate object). The same analysis would apply in the same way to a sentence like "lightning struck the tree." Here the predicate "struck" describes a property of or relationship between the two arguments, "lightning" and "tree." For logic, expressions like these—called propositional functions of two variables, $p(x1, x2)$—are statements that there are two sets, X1 and X2, that x1 belongs to X1, that x2 belongs to X2, and that for any ordered duple (x1, x2) belonging to the product set X1 × X2, the propositional function is true or false.

I trust that the reader finds something odd about this characterization. In the first example (Hoyt remembered himself giving the speech), the "predicate" predicates an intentional relationship on an occasion between me, my mind, or my memory, and a proposition, the meaning of a proposition, or thinking a proposition. In the second example (lightning struck the tree), the predicate describes a relationship that cannot possibly be intentional—except by some anthropomorphic construal—between some lightning and a particular tree. As far as logic is concerned, the only difference between "Hoyt" and "lightning" or between "tree" and "my memory of my doing something" is that they are (constant) arguments, terms, or individuals that have arbitrarily been given different names and belong to different sets (don't ask me of what).

What these examples suggest is that predicates—for example, those that describe how a person experiences something—typify their objects in two-place predications, just as those that categorize subjects in one-place predications do. Further, they typify the subjects of those two-place predications. Predicates of cognitive attitude mutually typify both arguments that they take in two-place predications, such that (a) how the (human) subject experiences and (b) that which is experienced are made correlative.

caused by the #sun#, which is in turn caused by the **sun**.[4] Likewise, "Captain John Smith" (Pocahontas's lover) is caused by #Captain John Smith#, who is in turn caused by **person$_x$**, known conventionally by his proper name. But the following examples show this to be illusory. #Cicada$_x$# has the identity of an individual—that is, is the same individual even though it is, at time t_1, #caterpillar$_x$# and later, at time t_2, #moth$_x$#. My #grandfather's axe# (i.e., the axe that was my grandfather's) remains intentionally an integral individual, despite the fact I have replaced its blade twice and its handle half a dozen times, and my grandfather himself, were he alive, would not today acknowledge it as ever having been his. The #United States#—that is, that to which the "United States" makes reference—despite vast changes over the past two hundred years, is still the same intentional individual entity today as it was in 1776 and cannot be caused by the United States. Some people in our culture, I am assured, believe that individual identity or entityhood can exist across what others claim to be distinct biological specimens. Garry Trudeau's "Boopsie" (of Doonesbury fame) believes that in her former existence she was Marie Antoinette and any number of other people. (She remembers neglecting to wear eye shadow to the French Revolution!)

Now only in virtue of language—and despite all we know about perceptual processes—can there be a state of affairs where (a) Boopsie in 1990 and Marie Antoinette in 1790 are deemed the same individual, or (b) the sun today is or is not the same individual as the sun yesterday, depending on one's perspective, or (c) Mr. Smith is or is not the same individual today he was a year ago, depending on one's perspective. Likewise, any and all so-called abstract individuals—for example, #luminiferous aether#,

---

4. The following orthographic conventions will be used throughout the remainder of the text. An expression enclosed in quotation marks—for example, "time"—indicates that the term so enclosed represents one of its possible definitions or conceptions, typically given by some other expression in the language. An expression enclosed by crosshatches—#time#—is taken to represent some typical experience, which may be a typical speaker's typical experience glossed by the word. A word given in boldface type—**time**—is taken to represent some putative bit of actual reality that the word might signify or refer to in use.

#the Middle Ages#, #the pope#—require more than putative **luminiferous aether, the Middle Ages,** or **the pope** to explain their entityhood as individuals (see Lyons 1989 for an interesting but difficult discussion of the so-called concrete-abstract continuum of nouns and other nominals and their relationship to first- and second-order individuals as considered by philosophers).

Both Bertrand Russell and Gottlob Frege seemed strongly to imply that a necessary condition of real reference was a real **individual.** Russell observed (1905) that the phrases "Scott" and "The Author of Waverly," despite differences of sense, refer to the same #individual#. This is not wrong, of course, but it leaves the impression that coreference is something the brute facts of existence will explain. Frege (1974) likewise seems to assume this in his observation that "the morning star" has the same referent as, but a sense different from, "the evening star." This is not wrong either, but it presupposes that individuals, like **Venus,** are somehow direct deliverances of nature.

While there may be aspects of the perceptual process which create (perceptual) individuals out of a smear or welter of **stimulus bombardment,** as the Gestalt psychologists have shown, it is not clear how this is sufficient to explain either #individual# or "individual." The world, natural cum cultural, does not in any obvious way exhibit or create identity, uniqueness, or necessary conditions for the existence of "individuals" and probably most of the #individuals# we daily talk about.

The freedom, in principle, to deem and justify any collection of experiences as a specific #individual#, and therefore the empirical possibility of an "individual," depends on an idealizing, usually conventionalized intention that necessarily distinct, nonidentical #experiences of individual X# are in fact nonetheless experiences of the same #individual X#, and not experiences of #X distinct individuals#.

Another way of making these same observations is to note that categories are almost always contained in or typified by still larger or subsuming categories. A question therefore arises, what kind of category might contain only "bedrock" **individuals** in the sense defined? The answer is that no such categories exist, because all putative **individuals** are in fact collections of #individual experiences#, and all #individuals# are reducible, at least in some sense, to collections of #nonidentical experiences#. So what limits continuous reduction or regression and prevents a kind of continuously reductive logical atomism? Practical reason; cultural, including occasionally "scientific," typification; and quite probably the human *"Bauplan."* Justification of the existence of #individuals#—that is, the placement of distinct experiences into the category "individual"—depends on many of the same cognitive faculties as justifications of the placement of #individuals# into "categories," thereby making them "individuals." Empirically this means that among the properties that any putative #individual# will be deemed to possess are those traceable to the categories this individual occupies. For both these reasons, a theory of categorization should account for the conditions of possibility for the existence of "individuals." We do not require a separate account of "individuals" to proceed with an account of categorization, precisely because the concept "individual" is a kind or type entailed by the concept "category."

Whether empirically the existence of individuals owes more to perceptual information—for example, simple ostension or pre-predicative experience—than does the existence of "categories" of individuals is an open question for which I have no general answer and for which there may be no general answer. In any case, a natural basis in #individuals# for "individuals" is no more obvious or likely than a natural basis in #kinds# for "categories."

Any adequate theory of meaning must provide an account of meaning invariance. The premier problem for rationalist approaches lies in their continuous, unacknowledged appeal to experience (culture, cognition) to account for what people are supposed to know analytically—solely in virtue of the innate, autonomous, modular semantic component of their language. The problem for empiricist approaches consists in their inability to describe coherently how humans' interaction with the "causal structure of the world" is directly represented in the semantics of language, unmediated by thought, belief, or knowledge, which presuppose language and without which there would be no human interaction with the world to begin with.

The approach of a phenomenological semantics is to argue that meaning in language—its semantics—is constituted of, and is therefore necessarily about, human experience, not in the empiricists' sense of sensory apprehension or observation (Carnap 1966) but in the "phenomenological" sense of how the world, including the "self," is posed for and presented to the embodied, enculturated being that lives it and lives in it. Operationally, this approach to meaning seeks to understand categorization or typification in terms of human cognitive and cultural experience and conversely seeks to understand cognition and culture in terms of categorization.

In our discussion of even such seemingly simple categories as "over," we saw how complex and subtle were its experiential typifications. Specifically we saw that what and how "over" signifies was not traceable to some objective material state of affairs, **over**. There was no need to ask the question what **over** actually is, much less to postulate that some existent kind or state of affairs, **over**, causes the experience #over#, which is in turn expressed by a separate concept, "over." Rather, the term *over* expresses a complex set of experiences, #over#. The meaning of "over" simply is #over#. The experience #over# is expressed as "over."

With reference to our central concern, time, a phenomenological approach obviates the need to ask (1) what is **time,** (2) how does it cause #time#, and (3) how does the concept "time" succeed in referring to either #time# or **time**? Rather, we ask something much more straightforward and answerable: how do we discover in pertinent linguistic expressions experience(s) of #time#?

CHAPTER THREE

The Spatialization of #Time#

We turn now to the question just posed and to another method-ological one, to which the remainder of the book is devoted: (1) What kind of experiences do ordinary linguistic expressions of "time" in any language and culture express, and how do they succeed in doing it? and (2) By what methods are we to discover answers to these questions and demonstrate convincingly that they are valid?

There is a school of thought within linguistic semantics which argues that semantic meaning can be understood as based upon or derived from our "crude" experience of space or spatiality. The basis for meaning invariance in this view lies in (1) the way in which humans, irrespective of culture, experience space, (2) how language expresses that experience, and (3) how language ab-ducts it to constitute other meanings/experiences. If it could be shown that the human experience of space is, in some substantial way, universal and that language appropriates that experience by processes that are themselves universal, then we would be on our way to explaining at least the conditions that make possible universal experiences of time and perhaps the bases of meaning invariance itself.

In his magisterial study of semantics, John Lyons has given a widely cited statement of this "localism" thesis, paraphrased here. By "localism," Lyons means

> The hypothesis that spatial expressions are more basic, grammati-cally, [syntactically,] and semantically, than various kinds of non-spatial expressions. . . . Spatial expressions . . . serve as templates for

other expressions . . . [because] spatial organization is of central importance in human cognition. . . . At its weakest the localist hypothesis is restricted to the incontrovertible fact that temporal expressions in many unrelated languages are patently derived from locative expressions. . . . The spatialization of time is . . . obvious and pervasive . . . in the grammatical and lexical structure of . . . many of the world's languages. . . . There is an obvious parallel between spatial and temporal deixis. As 'here' and 'there' can be analyzed as meaning 'at this place' and 'at that place' respectively, so 'now' and 'then' can be analyzed as meaning 'at this time' and 'at that time.' (1977:718, 724)

Lyons goes on to describe the analogical affinities between "movement of someone or [some]thing from one place or source, via some path, to some destination or goal" and such various two-place predications as "coming to know," "going to sleep," "causation" (bringing about), "implication" (deducing one thing from another), "manner" adverbials (do it "this way"), coming into "possession," and of course "existential" (there is/are) constructions (Lyons 1977:720–24).

Leonard Talmy has written a series of important papers in which the semantic expression of the crude experience of space (and motion) serves as data for examining how different languages schematize or structure such experience (Talmy 1975, 1978, 1983) and how such comparative study leads to general principles for how language maps fundamental semantic meaning-bearing entities into words and expressions in surface structure (Talmy 1985).

In a kindred vein, Traugott (1975, 1978) has sought to document in cross-language study the degree to which the crude experience of space constitutes a parameter or template for the structuring of time, tense, and aspect in human language. Psychology has weighed in with concordant views in the work of Eve Clark (1971, 1973), Herbert Clark (1973), and George Miller and P. N. Johnson-Laird (1976). Several major ethnographies have organized general cultural description around ideological and institutional schematizations of space and their role as template in the structuring of other experience, especially that of time—Beidelman (1963) for the Kaguru; Givens (1977) and Witherspoon

(1977) for the Navajo; Keesing (1991) for the Kwaio; Mandal (1968) for India; Needham (1965) for classical China; Ortiz (1969) for the Tewa; and Thornton (1980) for the Iraqw.

This literature shows that in human language there is evidence for a "spatialization" of time and of numerous other experiential domains. For example, in English, in which locative formatives are expressed as free lexical morphemes (prepositions), we can readily discern the locative force of predications (typifications), even of something seemingly so lacking in spatial significance as mental acts/states. For example, one "looks into," "looks over," "thinks through," "wrestles with," "talks about," "comes upon," "stumbles over," "runs up against," "returns to," "goes into," or "runs away from" a problem. Linguists seem to agree that somehow the experience of space comes ontologically and developmentally before experiences in other domains, which, by means of language, are informed by the primal experience of space itself.

Jackendoff formulates this notion cogently:

> The semantics of motion and location provide the key to a wide range of further semantic fields. . . . The significance of this insight cannot be overemphasized. It means that in exploring the organization of concepts that, unlike those of #physical space#, lack perceptual counterparts, we do not have to start *de novo*. Rather, we can . . . adapt . . . in so far as possible the independently motivated algebra of spatial concepts to new purposes. The psychological claim behind this methodology is that the mind does not manufacture abstract concepts out of thin air. . . . It adapts machinery [the experience of space] that is already available. (1983:189)

> Any theory of the structure of language is ipso facto a theory of the structure of thought. . . . All [events] and [states] in conceptual structure are organized according to a very limited set of principles, drawn primarily from the conceptualization of space. . . . This structure is cognitively induced: one could not decide to abandon thematic structure for some other organization. It defines the terms in which any kind of discourse, literal or metaphorical, must be framed. (1983:209)

Implicitly, Jackendoff reasons that there is an experiential datum, #space#, called "space" which is pretty much the same for all peoples and cultures. Different languages may "dot" with words the semantic space of #space# a bit differently, but basically they each wind up covering the same ground, as it were. This makes good sense. After all, any culture that became stubbornly fanciful about space and its matter and energy occupants would be set on a parlous course.

In regard to indefinitely many other experiential domains including that of #time#, linguists reason that one knows what the language of "time" expresses, not because one has, or even can have, an experience of #time#, but because one uses one's experience of #space# to constitute (and express) one's experience of "time." The inchoate experience of time (and many other experiential domains) is supplied from experience of space that is already there. Thus spatial experience serves as a homology of, or analogy for, what we can't quite "put our fingers on"—#time#.

To test the validity of this claim, one must satisfactorily deal with the following issues:

First, we must postulate or discover just how language's use of words that express the experience of space contribute sense to words that express the experience of time. That is, we must postulate or discover the specifically spatial experiences that are transferred or imported into the domain of time by virtue of the "spatial" words that make this transfer. Statements that time is experienced in terms "analogous," or "parallel," to that of space, while suggestive, are also rather vague.

Second, we must postulate or discover which components or aspects of the experience of space, the experience of time, and the processes of typification/categorization of the one by the other are open to, and are therefore expressive of, specific, culturally contingent institutions and conditions of knowledge. Contrariwise, we must discover which aspects are culturally invariant and "cognitively induced," despite cultural/linguistic differences of experience in these domains.

Third, we must postulate or discover how best to conceive of the domain of #time experience# such that cross-language/culture comparisons are truly commensurate. Experience is basically categorial, and categories are invariably constructed from many experiences other than what can be perceived or inductively distilled from the tokens that a category comprehends. All categories presuppose background conditions of belief or knowledge, which always contain, in turn, a preponderance of culturally specific content.

To establish that domains of experience in different languages/cultures are in some important sense cognate, we must translate culturally particular belief systems without unwittingly bending them to fit one particular language's/culture's lexical sedimentations or categories. We must identify in as culturally/linguistically unbiased a way as possible a formal object, "experience of time," into which specific #time experiences# of different cultures/languages can be translated, thereby rendering them theoretically cognate—instances of a theoretically justified metacultural category, "time."

Fourth, we must ascertain the extent to which the localist hypothesis has been powerfully but inefficaciously informed by our own cultural preoccupations with it over the past twenty-five hundred years. Within our cultural tradition alone, many different conceptions of space and time have been formulated. We cannot simply decree that some one of them constitutes an appropriate metacultural framework and use it as the criterion for discovery of cognate experience in any language/culture. We must avoid reification of our own experience, its elevation to the status of perceptual/conceptual universal, and valorization of it because we happen to find it manifested in other languages/traditions.

THE CENTRAL HYPOTHESIS

In light of the arguments made above, we recast the three opening questions as terms in a hypothesis: if (a) the experience and therefore the linguistic expression of crude space is universal (invariant across languages/cultures) and if (b) the *process* of typifying nonspatial experiential domains in terms of spatial ones is invariant across languages/cultures, then (c) the linguistic expression of the experience of time will also have a universal, invariant component or aspect across languages and cultures.

Three requirements must be met to test this hypothesis and deal at the same time with the four confounding issues noted:

1. The cultures selected for comparative study should be characterized by very different beliefs, knowledge, and institutions so that one minimizes the chances of mistaking for universal characteristics of #time# those arising from the chance similarity of beliefs or institutions, or from the fact that a characteristic may be accidentally common to a sample of languages/cultures.
2. A set of language-specific data, whose form is nonetheless a linguistic universal, must convincingly represent or express those metaculturally justified temporal experiences.
3. An analysis of those language-specific data must be undertaken to reveal the degree to which the intra- and cross-language/culture variation in the expression of temporal experience can be associated with (a) linguistically constant (universal) expressions/experiences of space and (b) linguistically/culturally variable and particular expressions/experiences, whether spatial or not. Degree of support for the spatialization hypothesis would be a function of the degree to which the character of the linguistic data can be reduced to, or explained by, (a) and, conversely, the extent to which (b) is nonexistent, is uncorrelated with, or is derivative of the dependent variable.

In this chapter we have stated: (1) to the extent that some prepredicative universal experience of space is the one or major template for the experience of time, then the expression in language of temporal experience should exhibit universal aspects; (2) irrespective of how space may be constructed or metaphorically used, to the extent that the experience of time is a precipitate of culturally contingent experience, we would expect language-specific expressions of temporal experience to be noncoincident and to map directly onto their cultural matrix of belief. Obviously, therefore, only by means of controlled cross-language and cross-cultural comparison can we test these premises of the spatialization hypothesis.

#Time# would seem to be an experiential domain in which the force of putatively primitive spatial experience and spatial analogy could most readily and unambiguously be ascertained. Unlike domains such as "property possession," "type identification," "predication of existence," "causation," and "bodily sensations," which are only experienced in terms of elaborate cultural models, rich perceptual experience, highly varied instantiation and exemplification, conscious attention, consideration, reasoning, and discourse, "time" (at least in its folk conceptions and apperception) would seem to be somewhat dependent on the structure of the spatial analogue as the source of its experiential properties. What domain more than that of time seems to lack phenomenal autonomy, boundedness, determinateness—to be a function of imagination, postulation, or merely of the stream of consciousness itself? What more than time is, like space, so familiar by encounter and yet, like space, so strange upon reflection? If we are to grasp what it means linguistically to experience and to explain causally one "meaning" by means of another, then "time" would seem like an ideal effect, or dependent variable, and "space" an ideal causal or independent variable.

CHAPTER FOUR

Linguistic Method for Cross-language, Cross-cultural Study of Time: Collocation and Metaphor

The spatialization hypothesis asks how essentially, inherently, and exhaustively the construction of space modally categorizes/ typifies the construction of time. Any answer requires establishing how the experience of #time# is linguistically expressed in a given language/culture. What, then, should be our data—that corpus of linguistic phenomena which would express both universal and culturally contingent categorizations or typifications of "time"?

For very straightforward reasons, two kinds of data will *not* do: morphosyntactic forms and individual lexical morphemes. Morphosyntactic forms have no determinate experiential counterpart, and second, most of them are not universal but are found variously in the surface structure of different languages. For example, some languages express tense derivationally; others do not. Still others do not express tense in any derivationally simple way at all. Some languages have adjectives; other languages do not. Most languages have a category of noun; a few do not. Some have morphologically signaled case systems; others do not. Some signal spatial information by use of free lexical forms; others use bound locative formatives. And so on.

In regard to individual lexical morphemes, as we have seen in our discussion of Leach's work and in our discussion of *over*, languages may map experiences onto words in quite varied fashion. But this does not per se show that the mapping function corresponds to, or creates, distinct language-specific categories of experience. In general, attempts to demonstrate cultural similarities or differences in experience by means of surface similarities or differences in such linguistic entities as morphosyntactic forms and word meanings are doomed to create a false image of limitless variability among languages and their speakers.

Wierzbicka in an intriguing work (1992) has attempted to get around this problem and get at linguistic and cognitive universals by means of a search for semantic "primitives"—the simplest, not-further-reducible atoms of human "thought" of which all languages would supposedly make use in building their respective lexicons. In this Leibnitzian approach, a set of innate universal (semantic) ideas serves to define other semantic concepts including those unique to particular languages/cultures. Although such semantic "atoms" may well exist, there are problems in using this method to investigate human experiential universals.

First, the number of experiential universals could vastly exceed the number of strictly semantic primitives. Second, the relationship between semantic primitives and extant word senses could well be extremely complex or even unpredictable. Third, the stock of extant word senses may not describe, or map in one-to-one fashion onto, culturally significant and patterned experiences. (Those interested in this approach to experiential universals through semantic primitives should consult Wierzbicka's book. We will not , for the reasons cited, go this route here in our study of time.)

So what kinds of categorial linguistic data might provide evidence of determinate experiences and at the same time be formal universals, thus permitting cogent cross-language, cross-cultural comparisons? Two—perhaps *the* two—that exist between the level of the word and the whole clause or sentence (and beyond to discourse) are *collocation* and *metaphor*. To appreciate, first, just how these constitute universal category-making linguistic processes that modally express determinate experience and, second, just how relevant they are to our investigation of the spatialization-of-time hypothesis, we must digress for an examination of each.

COLLOCATION AND CATEGORIZATION

That structure or process called collocation is neither a strictly syntactic-level nor a lexical/morphologic-level form; it exists, rather, in between the frozen syntax of sentences that compose the meaning of words and the open, largely generative syntax of ordinary sentences. What is it? For a person who lacks the linguistic and cultural competence of a native speaker of English, phrases like (a) "stubborn ox," "scared rabbit," "sly fox," "old maid," "proud father," "Jewish mother," "dirty tramp," "dumb blonde," "Commie symp," or (b) "smoke like a chimney," "swear like a trooper," "stare like a zombie," "drink like a fish," and "run like a rabbit" may seem like ordinary phrases.

But a native speaker knows them to be something more than this. They are clichés, idioms, or other stock phrases used irreducibly as epithets. The words go together in a more intimate way than the syntax would indicate. The inherency and durability of typification are greater than their syntactic structure of modification or predication alone would lead one to construe. For a person with native communicative competence, the noun head in list (a) in fact already contains the experiential association that the adjective adumbrates. The noun copies and therefore reasserts "features" of the adjective, such that the adjective loses much of its force as a preposed qualifier or predicate and melds with the noun itself.

Approaching the same issue from a somewhat different angle, T. F. Mitchell defines a collocation as "an abstract composite element which exhibits its own distribution [i.e., privileges of occurrence in syntactic structures]. [For example], men—specifically cement workers—work in cement works; others of different occupation work on works of art; others perform good works. . . . Good works are performed, but cement works are built and works of art are produced" (quoted in Bolinger 1975: 102).

Why, asks Bolinger (1975:102), do builders not produce a

building or authors invent a novel, since they invent stories and plots? Bolinger's question is most apposite, and the answer is, in general, that, as collocations reflect cultural patterning in the use, acquisition, and transmission of language, so they reflect the cultural patterning of knowledge, situation, and purpose, of which langauge is always, at least tacitly, expressive.

There is a *syntagmatic* (Firth 1957) dimension of meaning (meaning expressed in virtue of collocation). Mitchell notes of the word *heavy*, "Clearly there is no other lexical item in English regularly associated with all of the words: cold, blow, dew, soil, damage, damages, sarcasm, sky, drinking, breathing, make-up, hand, handed, crop, rain, work, lorry, gun, accent, fall, heart, features, top-spin, humor, hydrogen, meal, going, etc." (1971:51–52). Looking at collocation from the viewpoint of restriction of collocation, we observe in (British) English that "termination of employment is called defrock for priests, disbar for lawyers, cashier for military officers, expel for students, suspend for players, and sack for workers" (Mitchell 1971:54).

Examples such as these suggest that meaning in language has an ongoing as well as a contrastive (paradigmatic) aspect. There grow up dependencies among linguistic units beyond simple syntactic, subcategorizational, or "semantic feature" compatibility which arise from the dialogic context of language use. "So-called definitions or glosses in dictionaries are not seen as 'the meanings' of the entries to which they correspond but rather as a somewhat mixed-bag of essentially mnemonic extensions of the word entry, in which an attempt . . . is made at summing up the entry's distributional privileges of occurrence" (Mitchell 1971:41). "The formal value of an [linguistic] item depends closely on (a) other items present in the text and the constraints and dependencies observable between them, and (b) the transformability of the text" (Mitchell 1971:42). "Lexical particularities . . . derive their formal meaning not only from contextual extension of a lexical kind [e.g., semantic fields], but also from the generalized grammatical patterning within which they appear" (Mitchell 1971:48). Accordingly, "the division between morphology and syntax is . . . a great deal less clear cut than is often assumed and may even be otiose" (Mitchell 1971:47).

Bolinger extends Mitchell's claim to the level of the clause or sentence: "At present we have no way of telling the extent to which a sentence like 'I went home' is a result of invention and the extent to which it is a result of repetition, countless speakers before us having already said it and transmitted it to us in toto. Is grammar something where speakers 'produce' (i.e., originate) constructions, or where they 'reach for' them from a preestablished inventory?" (Bolinger 1961:381)

Collocations, then, are phrases that occur and recur in a given range of syntactic and discourse environments so frequently and with such fixed or stereotyped meaning that the ordinarily distinct contribution of the lexical items composing them is significantly suppressed. They are repeated linguistic units above the level of word. The repetition occurs, of course, within texts or discourse, so that much of what a collocation expresses is associations from its context of repeated use. So language use has direct effects on certain aspects of language form—that is, collocation or remembered bits of text or discourse and their context—which in turn must be indices of the cultural organization. Collocation is the only way to explain why in modern English we *bake* bread, cake, apples, fish, and ham, while we *roast* nuts, beef, lamb, and pork and can either bake or roast chicken and turkey. These collocations directly reflect and "index" culture history: the cuisine of (Germanic) Saxon England, the Norman invasion and its culinary impositions on courtly life, the peculiar sharing of chicken, and the late arrival of turkey (a New World fowl) into English.

Deborah Tannen has spoken of collocation as "prepatterning." "[Collocation] . . . constitutes part of the grammar of a language: not abstract patterns but actual bits of text which are remembered, more or less, and then retrieved to be reshaped to new contexts" (1989:37). Collocations exhibit, of course, varying degrees of "tightness," or what Tannen calls "fixity." That is, they are resistant in varying degrees to lexical substitution and syntactic transformation. Idioms, for example, exhibit such tightness of collocation that they verge on becoming single lexical items and therefore are closed to syntactic transformation.

Apropos of this, Bolinger asks a pregnant question: "If idioms can vary so widely in tightness, the question arises whether everything we say may be in some degree idiomatic—that is, whether there are affinities among words that continue to reflect the attachments the words had when we learned them, within larger groups" (1975:102). Tannen concurs: "Language is less freely generated, more pre-patterned than most current linguistic theory acknowledges" (1989:37). Citing Bolinger, she continues: "Many scholars . . . have pointed out that idioms are where reductionist theories of language break down. But what we are now in a position to recognize is that idiomaticity is a vastly more pervasive phenomenon than we ever imagined, and vastly harder to separate from the pure freedom of syntax" (1989:37–38).

Tannen gives a concise overview of the literature (1989:38–42), which manifests this "increasing attention paid recently to idiomaticity or prepatterning," so I shan't repeat it here. She notes some of the various terminology used to designate this phrasal prepatterning: formulaic expressions, phraseological units, idiomatic expressions, set expressions, conversational routine, routine formulae, routinized speech, collocations, and lexicalized sentence stems. In the field research described below, I have used more colloquial forms: stock phrases, sayings, proverbs, idioms, aphorisms, clichés, and the like.

This pervasive relative fixity of linguistic form above the level of the word and generally below the level of the sentence manifests directly the dialectal and dialogic relationship between language form and language use. Tannen (1989:42–43) cites commendations of this observation from such notables as Wittgenstein, Heidegger, and Bakhtin, the last of whom she quotes: "The living utterance . . . cannot fail to brush up against thousands of living dialogic threads . . . ; it cannot fail to become an active participant in social dialogue. After all, the utterance arises out of this dialogue as a continuation of it—it does not approach the object from the sidelines" (in Tannen 1989:43). I think this is Bakhtin's way of saying that many form-meaning pairings have an institutional status—they reflect cultural patterns of dialogue, belief, and action—so that the context of text or dialogue imparts significance to the repeated language forms embedded within it.

One of the effects of collocation, noted allusively above, is to induce a high degree of typificational inherency and durability in predication or the modification of arguments. That is to say, the collocation comes as a whole to express a category. To be sure this notion is precisely grasped, let me illustrate it with a couple of specific examples.

In English, preposed deverbal adjectives differ *certeris paribus* (i.e., controlling for the effects of collocation) from predicate adjectives or participles in terms of the degree of inherency or durability of the typification, modification, or predication imposed on the subject noun head.[5] "The typical perfect participle that can be used attributively [i.e., preposed to its noun head] is one that leaves its mark on something: a dented fender, a wrecked train, a bruised cheek, a frozen branch, a smudged eyelid. When one scratches one's head, the result is not *a scratched head. . . .

5. There are many ways, other than collocation, to induce typificational inherency or durability—that is, such that the predicate and its argument jointly express a single category. Obviously, converting a verb to a predicate adjective or to a noun does so, as we see in the sentences in the sets below.

(1) Tigers eat meat. (2) Tigers are meat-eaters. (3) Tigers are carnivores.
(1) Throckmorton fusses constantly. (2) Throckmorton is very fussy.
(3) Throckmorton is a fussbudget.
(1) Homer tells tales. (2) Homer is a teller of tales. (3) Homer is a talesman.

A predicate noun in English expresses a typification that is more inherent and durable than that expressed by a predicate adjective. Thus, in the following sentences, we deem the subject that a predicate noun subcategorizes to be more inherently, intimately, inalterably typified by that category than is accomplished by the corresponding predicate adjective.

is Norwegian	is a Norwegian
is black	is a black
is ungrateful	is an ingrate
is slovenly	is a slob
is foolish	is a fool

While we can express various degrees of typificational inherency by means of various syntactic structures and even lexical choices, we accomplish this end also by means of collocation—patterned language use. Moreover, collocation is a language universal—it is one way all languages have of inducing a typificational inherency of a predicate on its argument. (Adjectives are not a universal; nor can a semantic contrast always be drawn between adjectives that are preposed versus those that are postposed.)

We have labelled goods but not *sent goods,[6] dented bells but not *rung bells" (Bolinger 1967:9).

Bolinger continues, "If an adjective names a quality that is too fleeting to characterize anything, it is restricted (with that meaning) to predicative . . . position. The meaning of ready in 'the man is ready' is . . . excluded from *the ready man" (1967:10). "We can have a nearby building, . . . but not a *nearby man. We can have a near, close, or far corner, but not a *near, close, or far dog. . . . Only customary or regular actions can attributively typify something. We have fish-eating dinosaurs, rum-running bastards, and law-abiding citizens, but not *scrap-eating bears, leg-breaking men, or birth-giving women" (1967:12–13).

The potential categorizational or typificational durability required for preposed adjectives in English must be understood intentionally and against a background of custom and language use, not as some objective "state of affairs." One can willfully upgrade apparent inherency, intimacy, or durability of typification by taking adjectives that normally occur only in predicate position and preposing them. Advertisers do this very profitably. They give us such curiosities as doctor-recommended aspirin, available power steering, computer-sophisticated, and failed candidacies. This forced prepositioning of adjectives has yielded collocations in some cases, to the extent that the ordinarily fleeting event expressed by the predicate has become an inherent property of the noun head. The only way that being recommended by doctors can come to be seen as a constitutive feature of aspirin, so as to create a category "doctor-recommended-aspirin," which brand X can instantiate, is to say so over and over. This melding of word meanings reaches an obvious asymptote in the case of full-fledged idioms, where the underlying syntax becomes that of a single word, as in "a point in time" (from the algebraic number line) or a "window of opportunity" (from linear programming). Just as words express stable, schematized categories of experience, so in a weaker sense do collocations.

Collocational structures tell us something about the experien-

---

6. An asterisk preceding an expression indicates it is not semantically or syntactically well formed.

tial world (i.e., the categorizations and typifications) in which language is used and which it is about. Collocation (or language prepatterning) constitutes expressions of the cultural patterning of language use and acquisition and therefore reflects or "parallels" (background) conditions of belief, dialogue, and other social action. Collocation or prepatterning is created in and reflects its cultural context of use far more directly and expressly than do the collected senses of single lexical items (recall our discussion of *over*).

As we will see presently in our study of collocations incorporating "time," transcultural universals of experience, to the extent they are manifest in culture and expressed, should lead to the appearance of universal collocations.

CATEGORIZATION BY METAPHOR

The second linguistic process of categorization/typification which we must examine, companion to collocation, is metaphor. The vast literature on this subject may suggest that no further examination is called for, as nothing new can be said. Let me immodestly risk trespass on the reader's indulgence by describing aspects of metaphor which, to my knowledge, have not been widely or carefully noted. The first aspect or attribute that is crucial to our investigation of time is called by the unfortunate term "syncategorematicity." This denotes a syntactic context in which words' senses do not enter into the composition of sentence meaning as constants but contribute to it in virtue of a change or augmentation of the given word's sense, traceable to the particular companion words and the syntactic context. Syncategorematicity violates assumptions of "compositionality," which postulates that words' senses are fixed in number and are independent (except for selection of sense) of syntactic/semantic organization.

We can gain an intuitive understanding of syncategorematicity by means of simple examples.

Consider the sets of sentences below.

Hoyt is a/an ———— artist.
Hoyt is a/an ———— spouse.
Hoyt is a/an ———— person.
eager
appalling
lazy
inattentive
important
meticulous
blind
mature
colorful
busy
New York

Ordinary set-theory–based logics would represent all the sentences formed of these various adjectives and nouns as having the same logical form. Without the notational devices, it would be something like:

hoyt ((NOUN (hoyt) and ADJECTIVE (hoyt))
(i.e., hoyt is such that he is NOUN and he is ADJECTIVE).

Obviously, this logical rendering fails to capture the fact that "artist," "spouse," and "person" are not #things# but complex concepts with syntactically complex underlying semantic representations, as are the various "adjectives." The ADJECTIVE + NOUN combinations given above "latch onto" one another in distinctly different ways, despite the common surface syntax. The only pairing of this list which comes close to the extensional meaning in predicate logic is "blind + NOUN" (i.e., hoyt is such that he is blind, and he is an artist/spouse/person). But even this is crude, for being blind and being an artist (e.g., such as a painter) are not understood as simple contingencies, as would, say, being a "male artist" or a "blind person."

The sense of the adjective shifts or changes by supplying for the noun head the terms "artist," then "spouse," then "person." One could be "appalling" as an artist but not necessarily so as a spouse or as a person, and the behavior that qualifies as "appalling" vis-à-vis art would not likely be coincident with the behavior that would be "appalling" vis-à-vis marriage or vis-à-vis one's human worth. "Importance" exists solely because of the evaluations of others—that is, their evaluations make importance. Being "blind" is not a condition created solely by others' evaluations. "New York," vis-à-vis art, is a categorization of one's method, genre, or *oeuvre*; vis-à-vis a person, it is a categorization of one's residence. "Mature," vis-à-vis art, is a categorization of one's accomplishment and growth in producing or performing the art; vis-à-vis a spouse or person, it seems to be a euphemism (required only in Western culture) for old.

Syncategorematicity means that the salient characteristics of the individual or "token" depend on the manner in which it is being typified, and conversely, the manner in which something is being typified depends on the salient characteristics of the "token." Said differently, syncategorematicity means that typification arises from an interaction of particular "token" and "category" or "type" characteristics in specific linguistic contexts of modification or predication.

In conventional syncategorematic typification, the interaction can be described in terms of some straightforward but underlying aspect of one's stereotyped experience of the constituents in the structure of modification. For example, the behaviors suggested by the phrases "good soldier," "good priest," and "good milch cow" are quite different because of great differences in our experience of the roles or notions of "soldier," "priest," and "milch cow," respectively. The same is true for the pairs "deep puddle"/"deep lake," "New York artist"/"New York resident."

But an important case of syncategorematic typification occurs where there exist no conventional understandings of how to project or to experience the characteristics of the "token" which are to be typified by particular characteristics of the "type." Conversely, there exists no conventional understanding of how a "token" instantiates a "type."

Where syncategorematic interaction involves such novel—as opposed to culturally conventionalized—typification, we have a living, sometimes potent, metaphor that invites or requires continuous interpretation. That is, it invites or requires experimental mappings of the "token" into the "type." If and when a given interpretation becomes normative or conventional, we have a dead metaphor, manifested as an extended or augmented sense (i.e., characteristic of the experience) of the "type," the "token," or both. In this way, language appropriates and lexically sediments novel experience as conventional word senses, which are the storage of normatively interpreted sentences. Lakoff and Johnson (1980) and Lakoff (1987) have made this point convincingly.

What Max Black (1979) has dubbed and allusively described as "metaphoric interaction" is in fact the general process of syncategorematic interaction applied to tokens and types such that the typification cannot be projected or experienced as determinate or conventional and so requires ad hoc, novel, and sometimes multifarious projections as novel experience. In the case of metaphor, the general and pervasive syncategorematic process is not constrained by stereotyped aspects of the meaning or experience of the lexical items, including their "ontological" categorization. For this reason, interpretation requires more self-conscious effort, including, I would guess, real time for full appreciation if not comprehension.

All of this is very abstract, but because it lies at the heart of what we undertake in our study of the metaphors of time, I will illustrate these points with an extended discussion of a single example. Let's take an expression found as a proverb in many languages: "Time is the best teacher." The analysis to be demonstrated here can be applied to the five organizing metaphors that we will see universally categorize temporal experience: (1) time is a partible entity; (2) time is its effect(s); (3) time is a medium in motion; (4) time is a linear or orbital course; and (5) time is its ascertained kind or quantity. Hence I take considerable time here to show the method of analysis which informs how we will understand the data to be presented.

Formulaically, the expression Time is a/the Best Teacher (or alternatively, entity/effect/medium in motion/course/ascertained kind or quantity) can be understood as follows:

One intends (e.g., believes, imagines, considers)
TYPIFIES (#token# time), ("type" best teacher), which
  presupposes that
EXEMPLIFIES ("type" best teacher), (#token# time), and
  quite possibly
PROTOTYPIFIES ("type" best teacher), (#token# time)

How does the syncategorematic interaction work in this case of typification? There are four sets of experiences and several typifications/categorizations whose recursive[7] application can conveniently be represented as a "product" or "composition" function.

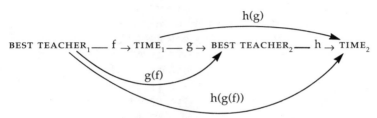

BEST TEACHER$_1$ represents the typical experiences of ordinary "type" BEST TEACHER; TIME$_1$ represents the typical experiences of ordinary #token# TIME. The function (f) is a mapping of these non-denumerably many experiences of the ordinary "type" BEST TEACHER onto those of ordinary #token# TIME. This mapping

---

7. "Recursive" means, roughly and informally, the capability to apply or make use of some rule on, or in terms of, the results of that (or a similar) rule's previous application. Phrase-structure rules are obvious examples of recursively applied rules, for their application produces an infinity of sentences made up of a finite number of phrase structures. For both rationalists and empiricists, word meanings (senses) are fixed a priori, whereas sentence meanings are gained by induction—that is, by recursive application of syntactic rules—calculating how sentences compose or combine the meanings of words to produce determinate sentence meanings. So, for example, the TOKEN "4" is included in the set of Even Numbers as "generated" by recursive application of three rules:

1. 2 ε EN,
2. If x ε EN, then x + 2 ε EN,
3. Nothing else belongs to EN.

creates a tension for two reasons: the experiences of typical "type" BEST TEACHER are not a subset of those of the typical #token# TIME, so a category-inclusion reading of the typification is blocked, and/or there are many experiences of the "type" BEST TEACHER which are (culturally) anomalous when predicated of #token# TIME. These understandings motivate two reinterpretations—actually, creations. First, TIME$_1$, as anomalously typified by BEST TEACHER$_1$ induces the creation of a new open-ended intentional object, "type" BEST TEACHER$_2$, represented by function (g). The function g(f) is the mapping of BEST TEACHER$_1$, as anomalously instantiated by TIME$_1$, onto the new intentional BEST TEACHER$_2$. Second, the anomalous typification of TIME$_1$ by BEST TEACHER$_1$ creates in addition a new intentional #token# TIME$_2$. This is represented by function h(g). The new "type" BEST TEACHER$_2$ typifies the new #token# TIME$_2$. This is represented by function (h). Finally, characteristics of original "type" BEST TEACHER$_1$ are mapped onto this new #token# TIME$_2$. This is represented by h(g(f)).

In sum, the functions map typification-rule applications into typification-rule applications. The entire product or composite function is the metaphor or metaphoric process.

Going through the functions one by one, we summarize the description just given:

(f) =	Best Teacher$_1$ TYPIFIES Time$_1$ <=> Time$_1$ INSTANTIATES Best Teacher$_1$
(g) =	Time$_1$ INSTANTIATES Best Teacher$_2$ <=> Best Teacher$_2$ TYPIFIES Time$_1$
(h) =	Best Teacher$_2$ TYPIFIES Time$_2$ <=> Time$_2$ INSTANTIATES Best Teacher$_2$
g(f) =	Best Teacher$_1$ EXEMPLIFIES Best Teacher$_2$ <=> Best Teacher$_2$ PROTOTYPIFIES Best Teacher$_1$
h(g) =	Time$_1$ EXEMPLIFIES Time$_2$ <=> Time$_2$ PROTOTYPIFIES Time$_1$
h(g(f)) =	Best Teacher$_1$ TYPIFIES Time$_2$ <=> Time$_2$ INSTANTIATES Best Teacher$_1$

Another way of conceptualizing this syncategorematic "inter-action" brings out another aspect of categorization/typification in metaphor, as presented in table 2.

Table 2

	BEST TEACHER (BT)		
	BT$_1$	BT$_2$	
TIME$_1$	a	b	(a + b)
TIME			
TIME$_2$	c	d	(c + d)
	(a + c)	(b + d)	

The letters a, b, c, and d stand for the joint intentional experiences of how the different TYPE Best Teachers typify the different TOKEN Times.

The difference between Best Teacher$_1$ and Best Teacher$_2$ is (a + c) − (b + d). The difference between Time$_1$ and Time$_2$ is (a + b) − (c + d). The difference between Best Teacher$_1$ and Best Teacher$_2$, as a function of whether it TYPIFIES uniquely Time$_1$ or Time$_2$, and conversely, the difference between Time$_1$ and Time$_2$, as a function of whether it is the argument that Best Teacher$_1$ or Best Teacher$_2$ uniquely typifies, is (a − b) − (c − d). The expression (a − b) − (c − d) is the *interaction* between specific intentional #Times# and specific intentional #Best Teachers#. The metaphor is the whole matrix, including the effects created by the "type" Best Teacher difference, those created by the #token# Times difference, and those created by the interaction of specific "type" Best Teacher with specific #token# Times. In any case, the typifications are "open"; the sets denoted by a, b, c, and d are not finite lists but represent intentional experiential objects, or, in Lakoff's terms, experiential gestalts. Because these are experiential objects, a nondenumerably large number of typifications can be made of each. This is what gives the experience of novel, compelling metaphor in language the quality of almost limitless interpretive richness.

Metaphor is the most important process in language for creating radically novel modality and therefore intentionality. Contrariwise, conventional, "literal" expression conveys prepatterned modality, which, unreflectively and mistakenly, we often understand actualistically or objectively. The distinction between the "literal" and the "metaphoric" is, in the view offered here, that between the conventionally typified and often prepatterned, on the one hand, and the novelly, creatively typified, and never prepatterned on the other. But the so-called literal and figurative are *equally* modal typifications, in that they represent experience in its intentional—that is, cognitively perspectival—sense.

What this assertion denies is that the literal and the metaphoric can be distinguished on the grounds that the "literal" is equivalent to the actual or possibly actual, while the "metaphoric" is equivalent to the anomalous, the impossible, or the merely modal. In our culture, for example, an expression like "the rocks cried out" will doubtless be understood as an intended metaphor, probably because we deem the property of being a kind or sort called "rock" and the property of being a kind or sort that "speaks" to be mutually exclusive "in nature." Thus we say that the sentence "the rocks cried out" is sortally incorrect but otherwise well formed, and therefore it meets—in the view of some, anyway—a necessary condition for a metaphor. Conversely, "literal" sentences are, if otherwise well formed, said to be "sortally correct."

The problem with using "sortal incorrectness" (Lappin 1981; MacCormac 1985) as a criterion for metaphor is identical to the problem of using transcendent truth condition as the meaning of sentences in general: "sorts"—like "truth conditions"—do not exist except as a function of belief, knowledge, and intention. In a culture such as that of the Navajo, where #rocks# and many other natural entities are deemed to be animate, to possess souls, and to communicate with people, the expression "the rocks cried out" may be sortally correct and therefore a literal—that is, a *conventionally* modal typification—even if for us in the West it is sortally incorrect and a metaphor—an *unconventional* typification. The literal is culturally preestablished, conventional modal typification/categorization, which, with repetition in language use, may well become sedimented in language form as collocation. The metaphoric is novel, unconventional modal typification/categorization that could not be expressed as collocation until the metaphor or system of metaphors dies and becomes a set of collocations.

With this experiential conception of meaning, we will be spared, in the study of time, quandaries created by the irrelevant, even misleading, issues of "truth," "reference," "contradiction," "literal paraphrase," "the imaginary," "the real," "sortal correctness," and the like. Further, the process of metaphor is revealed to be but a special use of a general semantic principle—syncategorematic typification—applied in the case of "types" (categories) and #tokens# or "tokens" (individuals) for which no tradition of past typification (and therefore no stored lexical senses) are available.

When the novel (metaphoric) syncategorematic typification becomes routinized in use—that is, becomes a collocation—the syncategorematicity may become less obvious as the words acquire, as new conventional senses, what started as experimentally interpreted senses. In this way, the lexicon is open to new experience and in time incorporates and sediments it as conventional word senses or as collocation. The lexicon, so conceived, is an open, dynamic process that records the cultural history of language use, including the changes that arise from bending language to new experience and experience to new language use—a viewpoint that Edie (1976), Bolinger (1980), Lakoff and Johnson (1980), and Tannen (1989) argue compellingly.

Metaphor does to the stock of lexically sedimented experience what theoretical science, literature, or any other critical thought does to the stock of culturally sedimented experience—break the extant types or typifications of experience (thereby assaulting the lexicon and common sense) and reorganize new, experimentally typified experiences into a different intentional synthesis. In time, the synthesis becomes routinized as at-hand, taken-for-granted experience coded in stereotypic lexical senses, texts, mathematical formulae, and so on. This concordance of metaphor and the collision of erstwhile incommensurate theories in critical science or other thought has often been noted (e.g., Hesse 1966; Boyd 1979; Horton 1970).

METONYM

Phenomenologically, metonym (the relations of parts to a larger whole) is based on a discourse about experience. So a "part" would be part of a discourse, not part of a thing or a sensation. This abstract point can be illustrated with our example "Time is the best teacher."

Consider the two typifying "discourses" elliptically given below.

TYPE	TOKEN
Characteristics of TYPE BT	Characteristics of TOKEN Time
(a) iterates	(a) iterates
(b) provides examples	(b) provides examples
(c) gives problems to solve	(c) gives problems to solve
(d) rewards/corrects	(d) rewards/corrects
(e) is long suffering	(e) is long suffering
(f) is continuously present	(f) is continuously present
(g) challenges anew	(g) challenges anew

This list could go on indefinitely. What is important is that the interaction of the "TYPE" experiences with those in the #TOKEN# experiences relies principally on existing, formerly metaphoric senses of polysemous words. The mapping does not simply create cognate experience: it relies on a stock of experience rendered cognate by preexisting metaphor itself. The mapping seems to be aided by the domains mapped, rather than being created by the metaphor *de novo*. There is a holistic—as opposed to compositional—process of meaning production at work here. The syncategorematic interaction of the domains in the "covering metaphor" provide discovery procedures for selection of constituent terms in each domain which can be mapped by use of already existing, but formerly metaphoric, extensions of the meanings of polysemous words. The particular senses of the polysemous words linked—indeed, melded—seem informed by the covering metaphor. Thus, "continuously present" does not have the association of physical contiguity in the case of Time, but it does in the case of Best Teacher.

Lakoff says that metaphoric mappings are motivated by the force of the source domain in preconceptual bodily gestural and spatial experience, and for him, the crude experience of space is the most fundamental source domain for metaphor. (We will return to this important claim in the next two chapters.) Thus "verticality" is the source domain for the target domain "quantity"—that is, "more is up, less is down." In another example, "source-path-goal," topography plus bodily movement along it is the source domain for the target domain "purpose." According to Lakoff, the force of these metaphors arises from early bodily experiences that are "correlated." Thus "more" is manifested as bigger and bigger piles of something, and we look to see rising piles. We crawl along to reach destinations, which become teleologically "purposes" (Lakoff 1987:288ff.).

There may be such kinesthetic, spatial, or other lived-body metaphors that are prepredicative in motivation (we will present good evidence for this below), but many perfectly good metaphors seem not describable as such. Some metaphors may involve mappings from very abstract, culturally constructed domains to very simple ones: "I'm counting on him." "Changing jobs has a significant opportunity cost." "He is marginalist in his outlook." "What's the bottom line here?" "An altruistic person is one who helps you maximize your utility function without expectation that that act will increase his own." "We live in a zero-sum society." Or, from a more engaging application of dismal science, we get: "He has an ace up his sleeve." "She gave me a fast shuffle or is dealing from the bottom of the deck." "You'd better not get lost in the shuffle or else have an ace in the hole." "You four-flusher!" "Let's lay our cards on the table." "What do we do when the chips are down?" "Stay with the blue chips." "How do they stack up against the penny-ante stuff?" "Well, they sweeten the pot by upping the stakes." "I'll stand pat." "Just play above board and don't pass the buck." "Otherwise you might wind up in hock." Some of Lakoff's prepredicative orientational metaphors appear as constituents in these metaphors from poker. But the game of poker is no more reducible to them than a wink is reducible to a blink.

The motivation and force of these metaphors—and probably most novel, compelling, apt ones found in great use of language—are irreducibly cultural. From experience in significant domains of cultural meaning and action can emerge the same force for metaphor as is, to be sure, found with prepredicative bodily experience. In short, metaphors do not need to be reduced to the prepredicative to explain force, and many metaphors, I would argue, are not so reducible at all. Metaphors of time, we shall see, present us with just this complexity: some are highly culture specific and referential to particular cultural contexts; others seem universal and referential to universal bodily experiences of space.

In the preceding chapters I have sought to establish the following points:

1. The meaning of words, phrases, and sentences in natural language is the expression of experience, and experience is fundamentally intentional.
2. Experience, so conceived, is expressed in the modal character of lexical or phrasal meaning (i.e., categorization or typification).
3. Culturally patterned language use imparts to linguistic units (e.g., words and phrases) a record of the meaning of that use in specific cultural and dialogic contexts; this use imprints itself in the form of collocations and once-novel metaphors that subsequently die and become new senses of words.
4. Metaphor is an example of syncategorematicity which breaks old modal categorizations/typifications and issues in new modal ones.

In the next chapters we substantiate these points with reference to the domain of "time."

CHAPTER FIVE

Time in Collocation and Metaphor

If there are transcultural universals of #temporal experience#, would these not necessarily be expressed in universal, cross-language collocations involving "time"? To answer this question, we require, of course, a large and random sampling of collocations that express temporal experience. By inspection and analysis of these data one can determine to what extent these collocations derive from more basic spatial expressions. Whatever items the collocations might contain—flectional morphemes, elements both of open classes (e.g., nouns or verbs) and of closed classes (e.g., formatives or prepositions), compounds, or idioms—their meaning would have to satisfy some metacultural criterion of temporal experience so that we can be confident we are making appropriate comparisons.

"TIME" DEFINED METACULTURALLY

The meaning (experience) of any entity depends upon how it is constructed. In the case of time, this will be some principle for definition, ascertainment, or measurement which is metacultural yet capable of subsuming that which is culturally contingent. The metacultural definition of time I shall use is experiential and relational and based on the conception advanced by P. J. Zwart (1976). Because of lack of space, I cannot digress to argue its merits against idealist and realist conceptions or show how it differs from the currently de rigueur formulations of an irreducible four-dimensional manifold of space-time, à la Minkowski (Margenau 1950). For scientific/technical discussion, debate, and justification of the view adopted, see Zwart 1976; or for an informal account, see Fraser 1987.

Definition: "Time" (i.e., that aspect of experience which is temporal) consists in the cognizing and conceptual linking of two or more sets of successive experiences—that is, experiences deemed to have a before-and-after relation. "Time" is a two-fold relation of (1) before-and-after succession within one set of experiences and (2) the (theoretical) linkage of two or more sets of such before-and-after experiences. The most fundamental and simple way in which this two-fold relation is cognized is in hearing ordered succession, especially the rhythm (or other phonetic events with apparent stochastic order) of human speech and song and the linking of two or more sets of such ordered-succession experiences. The faculty that senses time in this sense is that of hearing, though kinesthetic-tactile and locomotor apprehension is also possible in heartbeat, pulse, respiration, autonomic/sympathetic nervous activity, walking, clapping, or dancing. Note that, in the absence of relative motion or change of state, there is no direct (i.e., nonsymbolic) visual expression of temporality and that the auditory experience of temporality does not require visible or palpable relative motion or change of state. "Sets of successive experiences" or "experiences of succession" we in the West conveniently call "clocks" or clock events. The duration of an experience is simply the number of clock events of one clock as compared with the number of clock events of another clock. Time is a function of (1) the way one organizes experiences, such that they constitute a succession, and (2) the intentional linking of two such sets of successive events, such that one can say an event or event succession in one set is equal to N-events/event successions in at least one other set.

One of many ways of representing such a conception of time is by relatively uniform motion over a fixed distance—for example, the movement of the shadow of a sundial or the hands of a conventional dial-type clock or a uniform transformation of state (a fluid or particulate aggregate passing from a container like a water clock or hourglass). Historically and cross-culturally, most clocks are not manufactured but are simple successive events of nature or culture, appropriated conceptually so as to perform the "clock function"—for example, solar events, climatic events, animal behavior, rituals and festivals, succession of monarchs, feeding a campfire, coming of age, recounting the past, explanation in mythic narrative, and, most important, birth and death.

This is a minimal metacultural conception of time-as-understood. As described below, it is used in this study, not to classify experiences in different languages/cultures, but to aid in discovery of relevant collocational expressions, of which the study required a large and random sampling. Such a sampling for various languages would likely contain evidence bearing on several aspects of the spatialization hypothesis. First, in these collocations we might discern the extent to which they are based upon spatial concepts or experiences, and whether they manifest a universal shared core of expressions or vary idiosyncratically. By inference from our phenomenological conception of meaning, we might be able to determine the extent to which temporal experience among cultures is alike, and how temporal experience, as indexed by collocations, is informed by culturally particular factors.

As noted, to demonstrate genuine universality of expression, the collocations have to be drawn from languages spoken by people with very different institutions and beliefs to assure against the confounding possibility that observed similarities are caused by cultural features that are merely by accident shared in common. The four languages/cultures selected for this indicative study fully satisfy this requirement: American English, Mandarin, Hindi-Urdu, and Sesotho/Setswana. The experiences of #time# in the cultures of the Judeo-Christian/western European world, China, northern India, and Bantu-speaking Africa are as different from one another as any four such cultures currently happen to be. Moreover, these differences in worldview and cosmology are discernible, not just in the Great Traditions of critical thought and science, but in the daily lives—the Little Traditions—of ordinary people, whose speech has yielded our data.

Four of the methodological criteria set forth have now been satisfied. We have (1) a metaculturally defined object, "time," with the aid of which to discover (2) a set of language-specific data, whose form is (3) a linguistically universal process of typification (collocation and metaphor) found in (4) languages/ cultures with radically different beliefs, knowledge, and institutions that might affect temporal experience.

COLLECTING THE COLLOCATIONAL DATA

The data presented below were elicited from ten individuals: the author, and two native speakers of Mandarin, five of Hindi, and two of Sesotho. The non-native speakers of English each grew up in a community in which his or her native language was the dominant language. They did not acquire fluency in English until after adolescence.

The data were collected over several (five to eight) interviews and were elicited by my describing for each respondent, purely as a heuristic device, the conceptualization of time contained in the metacultural definition. I did not provide examples of collocations in English which I had earlier assembled, but I gave instead examples of certain words in English which might be found in such collocations: *instant, moment, soon, again, slow, fast, now, then, later, earlier, change, detain, accelerate, era, epoch, period, duration, hour, day, month, year, clock, calendar, tide,* and, of course, *time.*

I asked them to think of ways of expressing in their respective native languages various aspects, dimensions, or instances of the metaculturally defined temporal experience using stock phrases, aphorisms, sayings, figures of speech that they had frequently heard growing up. Given the practical necessity of working with multilingual informants, I tried every feasible technique to discourage them from thinking of and translating English exemplars into their native languages. Ideally, one would train these bilingual respondents as field workers who could then go to China, India, or Africa and work with monolingual speakers to collect the data from actual discourse. Interested readers could, of course, undertake this research in these or in other languages to check the reliability of my findings.

CATEGORIZATION OF COLLOCATIONS

The data are presented in terms of five categories obvious from first inspection of the data. These categories are based on the metaphoric terms that predicate of time a property or relationship. The initial classification proved remarkably precise and general, in that these same categories were equally to be found in expressions from all four languages.

To check the reliability and ease of my judgments in assigning collocations to the categories, I gave three subjects (students) a description of the root metaphor that I deemed to be common to the categories, as I discerned them from initial inspection of the data: (1) "time is a (partible) entity"; (2) "time is its effects"; (3) "time is a medium in motion"; (4) "time is (a) a linear course, or (b) an orbital course"; (5) "time is its method of ascertainment/ measurement"; and a sixth category, "don't know/can't decide." I gave the three all the collocations, including English translations of those in the "foreign" three languages. I asked them (independently, of course) to assign each collocation to one of the six categories. Each subject had to place each collocation in one, and only one, of the six major categories. (Collocations of space-time deixis were not dealt with in this classificatory check.)

The students couldn't understand some of the expressions, especially in Mandarin, because they lacked relevant background knowledge. For example, the notion of "shade" as a measure of time, the significance of a length of jade as a unit of value, and the movement of a shadow in a sundial escaped them. These and other expressions from Hindi and Sesotho they assigned to the "don't know" category. For the remaining collocations, however, the assignments showed in most cases 100 percent agreement with my initial intuitive ones.

There were exceptions to this 100 percent agreement. Where two raters assigned an expression to one category and two assigned it to another single category, the expression is entered in each one. Hence a given collocation can appear in more than one category, but this happened fewer than a dozen times in more than 600 sortings. Where an expression was deemed by at least two raters to belong to a certain category, and the other two raters disagreed, the majority assignment prevailed. Where the three students assigned an expression to the "don't know" category, my judgment prevailed. There were fewer than one dozen such cases among the 600 collocations. There were a few expressions in which three of the four of us were in agreement and one disagreed. This occurred 18 times in more than 600 sortings. No expression was assigned to four different categories. Excluding the "don't know" option, no expression was assigned to three different remaining categories. Although reliability does not entail validity, I interpret this extremely high reliability, along with other evidence to be described below, to suggest strongly that the categories constitute a *partitioning* of time experiences as these are collocationally expressed into almost mutually exclusive and probably exhaustive subsets.

All my respondents—that is, those who provided the data— agreed that the categories I devised and the assignments that the students and I made were valid on the face of it, made complete sense, were not arbitrary, and revealed important modalities in terms of which time is expressed in their respective native languages. None of the respondents claimed to have thought about the concepts, the categorizations (metaphoric predications), or the relevant collocations prior to working with me. All the respondents commented on how much the exercise made them acutely aware of precepts, values, beliefs of which they were at best dimly conscious. All expressed, at the outset of the work, how different the "conception" or "consciousness" of time is in their native culture compared with that of the United States. The respondents were very surprised by the data they themselves collected, which disclosed numerous commonalities among the data for all four languages. These observations add credibility to my claim that the procedure for eliciting the data did not so constrain the respondents that they were led to observations by tendentious elicitation or an obviously biased methodology.

It is unusual to present "raw" data in the body of a text, but I want readers with various language competences to be able to carry out their own analyses of these or cognate data from other languages and to be able to move back and forth easily between these data and the observations and generalizations made in the following chapter.

TIME IN AMERICAN ENGLISH

Below are listed nearly 150 collocations—idioms, aphorisms, clichés, figures of speech, fragments of proverbs, and words frequently co-occurring in everyday speech—which any native speaker of English would recognize as "stock phrases." Starred items are those not classified with 100 percent agreement.

List A. Time is a partible entity

spend time
divide time*
seize/catch the time/moment
waste (of) time
save time
have time
allocate time
apportion time
time is ripe

plenty of time
time to do X*
with the lapse of time*
some time*
pass the time
the age (of history)
the future is full
borrowed time

kill time
outlay of time
time is money
spare (one) time
do something with one's time
good/bad/fine/troubled time(s)
measure time*
fullness of time
time weighs heavy on one's
    hands
time out of mind
in good time
bit of time
against time
use one's time
the past is dead
steal time
time on one's hands

List B. Time is its effects

father time
time destroys
ravages of time
time is on our side*
time reveals/discloses

time-worn
time wears away
time conquers all
time heals
time and tide befall/betide (one)

List C. Time is a medium in motion

flow of time	time moves on
time is coming (when)	time is past
time has passed (one by)	time flies*
time goes/flows/slips/slides by	on the wings of time*
time is coming/approaching	time marches on
stop the march of time	time stood still
time waits for no one	time drags on/by
time races on/ahead	time lapsed (elapsed)*

List D. Time is a course

I. A linear course

look ahead (in time)	look into the future
look back in time	look into the past
X follows/precedes/succeeds Y in time	time is short
here and now*	then and there*
into infinity	time without end (eternity)
beginning of time	length of time
a long time	a short time
before (in time)	after (in time)
in front of us	face the future
behind time	ahead of time
during (between) times	at a time
in time	move ahead
go forward in time	
a point in time	in the nick of time
at the same time	once upon a time
in the beginning	in the course of time
at times	the end of time
over time	along in time
time warp	with time
for a time	distance in time
time stretches forth	from time to time
for all time	before the beginning of time

II. An orbital/circular course

life is a circle	the round of life
a wheel of fortune	ashes to ashes/dust to dust
time will come again	the seasons come 'round.
over and over again	the swift seasons roll
time and time again	time is over

III. Space-time deixis

events that are before me I will come to
events that have already happened are behind me
events that come/arrive later will follow me
events that are later I will come to
events that happened before, happened earlier, are behind me/
    I leave behind
what lies before/has yet to happen/is later/has yet to come to
    us/we face

List E. Time is its ascertainment/measurement

lose time	gain time
keep time	tell time
give time	count time
time to burn*	divide time*
mind time	time weighs heavy on one's hands
bind time	time flies*
slow down time*	speed up time*
moves/flows/goes/ on time	tight schedule
run out of time	time's up
	time waxes/wanes*
mark time	turn time around/backward/ ahead
turn back the clock	set the clock ahead
run on time	time runs slow/fast
early/late (relative to time)	in/on time
in the fullness of time*	the sands of time*

List F. Some nonspatial expressions of time

fast, rapid, slow, now and then, concluding, often, seldom, beginning, changing, again, earlier, waiting, moment, instant, sooner, later, delaying.

TIME IN MANDARIN

Below are listed more than 150 collocations in Mandarin expressing temporal experiences that fit our metalinguistic criteria. As is the case in the English list, this is not an exhaustive, but certainly is a more than adequate, sampling of the universe of relevant collocations.

Consistent transliteration has proven very difficult. In general I have tried to render everything in Pinyin, the modern system now standard and, I guess, favored in the People's Republic of China. One informant's work and much of the quoted material is in the Wade-Giles system, or in an ad hoc modification of that system. Although the reader is entitled to "correct" spelling, it is difficult to provide this for a language that has for thousands of years used a quasi-semantically based ideographic/pictographic writing scheme.

List A. Time is a partible entity

shijian	time-partition/space
yishi	lifetime
ji	twelve years, century, year
jiyuan	year beginning/first of era
yibeizi	lifetime
niantou	times
shijie	time segment
nongshi	farming time
gengshi	tilling time
zhongshi	planting time
xianshi	empty, unoccupied time
xiashi	leisure time

youshi	have time
feishi	cost, take time
zhanshi	brief time, temporarily
pianshi	slice (of) time
shishi	time-time (all the time)*
kongqian juehou	empty before break off after (never again)*
duoshizhiqiu	much troubled times
shiji	time (opportunity) to do X
shibukeshi	time (opportunity) not okay to lose
tian bujianian	heaven not lend (a) year*
jishi xingle	reach time have pleasure
jishi	reach/seize time
jinshi zhuofei	today right, yesterday wrong*
cunyin qianjin	inch (shade) time, thousand gold*
cunyin chibi	inch (shade) time, foot jade*
cunyin zixi	inch (shade) time, its own treasure*
cunyin nanmai cunguangyin	inch gold difficult buy inch light-shade (an inch of gold cannot buy an inch of time)
cunyin qianjin	inch shade/time thousand gold*
cunyin shijing	inch shade/time be fought*
cunyin shijing chibi feibao	foot jade not treasure, inch shade/time fought for*
liangshi jiri	auspicious time/day
jiri liangchen	auspicious day/hour
dahao shiguang	very good (light) time
deshi	obtain favorable time
shi shi	lose/miss time
cheng shi	ride time/seize moment
yingshi dangling	answer match time
feng shi	meet time/season
he shiyi	fit/suitable time
shiji chengshu	time opportunity ripe

zhuajin shiji	grasp tight time opportunity
shiqu shiji	lose gone moment

List B. Time is its effects

shiling	time ordering/causing
shiji	favorable time/opportunity
shishi	time condition/tendency
shibi	current time evils/fraud
shiyu	time praise/fame
shiyun	time fate/luck/fortune
nianlao	time-worn
shibuwoyu	time not me wait
suibuwoyu	year/age not me wait
shijian buliuren	time interval not keep man
shiguang buliuren	time light not keep man
shijian buraoren	time interval not spare man
guangyinburaoren	light/shade (time) not spare man
suiyueburaoren	year/month not spare man
shu wang zhilai	count gone past, know coming future
shishi suoqu	trend/tendency of the time
shishi bujia	time trend not good

List C. Time is a medium in motion

congqian	go before/in front of
quri	gone day
wangri	gone day
lairi	come day
shijian liushi	time flow gone
shijiande jiaobu	time's footstep (pass away)
su	fast moving of time
chi	slow moving of time
guangyin sijian	light shade (time) like arrow*
riyue rusuo	day/sun/moon/month like shuttle*

baiju guoxi	white colt pass crack (glimpse of fleeting time)
fuguang lüeying	fleeting light/shadow (time)
shihuo guangyin	stone spark light/shade (time flickers out)
shilai yunzhuan	time come fortune turn*
shihou daole	time season come already
shihou weidao	time season not yet arrive
shiguo fengyi	time gone/passed, wind change
wuhuan xingyi	things change, stars move
chidao	slow arrive (late)*

List D. Time is a course

I. A linear course

qian	before/in front of (time)
hou	after/behind (time)
xianzai	appear present (to eye)
xianshi	now/present to eye (time)
muqian	eye before/front (now)
congqian	before, in front of (time)
qianshi	before time (formerly)
suishi	follow time (anytime)
shixian	time limit
like	stand hour/mark (immediately)
jishi	this time (here)

II. An orbital/circular course

yinian you yinian	one year again one year
yitian you yitian	one day again one day
yiri you yiri	one sun again one sun
niansui diegeng	year-year in turn exchange/ substitute*
yiyang laifu	one spring come return again
yiyuan fushi wanxiang geng xin	one beginning again begin myriad image renew

riri yeye	sun/day sun/day night night*
xingshuang lüyi	star frost repeatedly move
xingyi douzhuan	star move constellation turn

III. Space-time deixis

shijian	time partition (space)
guangyin	play of light shade and shadow = time
cong . . . qi/kaishi	from . . . beginning (space and time)
cong . . . dao	from . . . to (space and time)
qian	before/previous/earlier/in front (space and time)
qiantian	before-day (day before yesterday)
qiansheng	previous lives
qianbian/tou/mian	front side, end, face (space only)
hou	after/later/behind (time and space)
houtian	day after tomorrow
houshi	later life/generation
houbian/tou/mian	behind, back side, end (space only)
shang	above/up/top/before/previous (time and space)
shangwu	forenoon, morning
shanggeyue	previous/upper month
shang yi beizi	previous/former life
xia	below/down/later/future/next/after (time and space)
xiawu	afternoon
xiageyue	below/following month
xia yi beizi	below/following life
xia dai	next/below generation
zuoyou	left-right/about (space and time)
jin	near/close/recent (time and space)

yuan	far/distant (time and space)
cishi cidi	this time this place (here and now)
suishi suidi	anytime anyplace
wushi wudi	no (particular) time no (particular) place = (anytime)
daiyuan nianyan	generation distant/far, year disappeared
tianchang dijiu	heaven long earth lasting

Events that have already happened are those that are before (*yiqian*) or have passed (*guoqu*) the experiencer/speaker.

Of the events that are before—that is, have already passed the experiencer/speaker—those that were experienced earlier (*xian*) are before/in front of (*qian*) those that were experienced later/after (*hou*).

Events that have not yet happened to the experiencer are those that will come (*jianglai*) or are yet to come (*weilai*).

Events that will come or are yet to come are all later or after/behind (*yihou*) the experiencer.

Persons of the upper—that is, former, previous times (*shang*)—are members of one's before or earlier (*xian*) generations.

Persons of the lower—that is, later times (*xia*)—are members of one's after/behind (*hou*) or later (*wan*) generation.

List E. Time is its method of ascertainment/measurement

tongshi	same (simultaneous) time
shiling	time ordering
shijie	time segment*
nianling/nianchi	age-teeth*
anshi	according to time
zhunshi	accurate time
shoushi	keep on time
wushi	mistake/miss time
wudian	miss dot/mark/point (on dial)
yidun fan de gongfu	a meal's time
yi dai/zhi yan de gongfu	a cigarette's time
yizhan cha de gongfu	a cup of tea's time

qianqiu wansui	thousand autumn, ten thousand years
tianchang dijiu	heaven long earth lasting
dilao tiaohuang	earth old heaven bound*
shi shi dai dai	generation after generation
yongchui qiangu	forever pass down*
yiri sanqiu	one day, three autumns
geng	shift/turns/watch
dageng	night watch drum (beat time)
baogeng	report/tell/announce night watches
gulou	drip/run/leak (head of *clepshydra*)
baoshi	report/tell time

List F. Some nonspatial expressions of time

Expressions based on experience of change or rhythm: *kuai* (fast with "heart" radical), *man* (slow with "heart" radical), *nianqing* (year light in weight, young), *nianzhang* (year grown, old), *dai* (generation).

HINDI-URDU TIME COLLOCATIONS

Below are nearly 150 collocations, mostly in Hindi, but some in the closely related dialect Urdu as spoken in Delhi. Again the problem of transliteration into Latin script is difficult. Different informants provided different spellings. There are historical (Sanskritic), ethnic, regional, and class-based variations in dialects which are associated with different writing conventions. In the face of considerable variation among informants, I have accepted one native speaker's editorial judgments on spelling.

List A. Time is a partible entity

samay bitaana	pass time
waqt lagaana (Urdu)	devote/take time

waqt baant'naa	distribute or allocate time (not a collocation)
aek pal	a moment (borrowed from English)
waqt barbaad karnaa (Urdu)	to waste time (lit. "destroy time")
samay kam haey	there is little time
samay nasht' karnaa	waste (destroy) time
makkhee maarnaa	kill flies ("kill time")
samay kee bachat	saving of time
samay kaatnaa	to get through time
samay haey	have time; there is time
samay naheen haey	not have time; there is no time
samay nikaalnaa	find time (to do X); to consult astrological charts for an auspicious time
ab waqt/samay naa rahaa	there is no longer any time
bahut samay/waqt haey (Urdu)	there is a lot of time
samay/waqt kee kameen naheen	there is no dearth of time
karney kaa samay/waqt haey (Urdu)	have the time to do X
yayh X karnay kaa samay/waqt haey	this is the time to do X
samay kee poorntaa/paripoorntaa main	in the completeness/fulness of time
kuchh samay	a little time; some time
thor'aa waqt (Urdu)	a little time; some time
waqt guzaarnaa (Urdu)	pass time
jhak maarnaa (Urdu)	kill time/waste time
meraa ayek aek minut' aek aek hazaar kee keemat rakhtaa haey	my every minute is worth a thousand*
samay/waqt ganwaanaa	to waste time
khaalee waqt (Urdu)	empty (i.e., "spare") time
samay/waqt kaa istamaal karo	make good use of your time
achch'ay din (Urdu)	good days (times)
achch'aa waqt	good time (to do X)
buray din (Urdu)	bad days (times)
burra waqt (Urdu)	bad time (to do X)

dukh kay din	days of sadness; hard days (times)
kat' hin samay	hard times
uchit samay par/main	at the appropriate time
samay kay saath	with time
samay kay viruddh	against time
waqt kay saath (Urdu)	along with time
waqt kaa istamaal (Urdu)	utilization of time; use one's time
samay kaa upyog	utilization of time; use one's time
maangaa huwa waqt (Urdu)	asked for ("borrowed") time
galat samay	the wrong/improper/ inappropriate time
theek samay	the right/proper time
uchit avsar	the appropriate occasion (time)
waqt kay saamnay sab jhuktay hain	everyone bows in front of time
su avsar say	good, auspicious arrival (time)
waqt ka faaydaa uthaanaa (Urdu)	to use one's time; "to profit from time"*
samay ka labh uthaanaa	to use one's time; "to profit from time"*
waqt say kyaa ladnaa	why fight time?
aeyk zamaanay main	in one time
bahut waqt/samay lag jaataa haey	a long time ago

List B. Time is its effects

jab samay aataahai, tabhi woh cheez hoti haey	when its time comes, only then does it happen
waqt tabaah kartaa haey (Urdu)	time ruins
samay naashak haey	time is a destroyer
samay sab khatam kar detaa haey	time destroys/ends everything
samay kaa koyee mukaablaa nahin kar saktaa	no one can compete with time
waqt kay nishaan (Urdu)	marks (ravages) of time
samay/waqt hamaaray saath haey	time is with us/on our side
waqt kay saath sachchaayee saamnay aa jaatee haey	with time truth becomes apparent; time reveals truth

waqt andhayraa door kartaa haey (Urdu)	time removes the darkness
waqt kay saath saath parda bhee uth jataa haey (Urdu)	with time, curtains too are lifted*
samay spasht karaygaa (educated)	time will clarify
waqt kay saamnay sab kee har hoti haey (Urdu)	time defeats all
waqt sabh ghaav bhar daytaa haey	time heals all wounds
samay main utaar chadhaav	time raises (lifts) and lets events fall

(N.B. One informant says there are too many idioms in this vein to collect, as "India is obsessed with the concept of the eternity of time destroying; time and its effect on life, especially the future, is our national pastime.")

List C. Time is a medium in motion

samay aa gaya haey	the (right) time has come
samay kay beetnay say	with the passing of time
waqt kay guzarnay say (Urdu)	with the passing of time
waqt kee dhaaraa	stream (flow) of time
samay kaa bahaav	flow of time
samay/waqt kay saath bayhnaa	to go with the flow of time
samay kee nadiyaa [nadee]	the (dear) river of time
samay beet jaataa haey	time passes
wah samay aa rahaa haey jab	that time is coming when
waqt usay peechay chod' gaya (Urdu)	time left him/her behind
waqt guzar jaataa haey	time passes
samay kay badhtay huay kadmon ko rok daynaa	stop the advancing steps of time
samay kissee kay leeyaye nahin rukta	time waits for no one
waqt kissee kaa intezaar nahin kartaa (Urdu)	time waits for no one
samay tayzee say aagay bad'h jaataa hai	time moves ahead with speed
samay aagay badhtaa hee jaata haey	time keeps moving on ahead

samay jaa/nikal/dhal chuka haey	time has already passed
waqt guzar chuka haey (Urdu)	time has passed
samay ud' jaataa haey	time flies
waqt kay bad'htay kadam ruktay naheen	time's advancing steps do not stop
samay nishchal khadaa rahaa (classical Hindi)	time stood still
samay maano ruk gayaa ho	as if time stood still
waqt mushkil say kat' taa haey (Urdu)	time passes with difficulty
X *karnay kaa samay aa gaya haey*	the time to do X has come
samay/waqt main aeyk lamhaa aataa haey	there comes a point/moment in time
jo waqt guzar gayaa, usay bhula daynaa	to forget the time that has passed
beetay samay ko bhula daynaa	to forget the time that has passed
bahut waqt guzar gayaa	a lot of time has passed
bad'ay din ho gaey	many days have passed
waqt/samay khatm/samaapt ho gayaa haey	time has run out
woh wakt/samay jaa chukaa	that time has already passed

List D. Time is a course

I. A linear course

(Note that there are very few, if any, collocations that predicate of time a linear or orbital linearity. Below are some collocations that are translatable into English expressions of linearity, but they make use of other metaphors.)

waqt thoraa haey	time is short
aagay daykhnaa	to see ahead ("think of the future")
bhavishya vichaarnaa	to ponder the future* (= previous phrase)

beetay samay ko daykhnaa	to look at the time that has passed
beetay huay kal ko daykhnaa	to see/look into the past
beetay huay samay kaa smaran karnaa	to study the time past
beetay samay par drishtee daalna	vision cast on time past
kaafee samay	long time (not a collocation)
thod'aa/kam samay	short time (not a collocation)
samay/waqt main taraqqi karna	to make progress (not a collocation)
samay/waqt main aagay badnaa	to move forward
bhootkaal par nazar daalnaa	cast one's gaze back into the past
samay/waqt kay dauraan	during the time
samay/waqt kay saath	with time*
samay/waqt main dooree/faslaa	a distant separation in time
beeta hua waqt wapis nahin aata	time that's past does not return
waqt main lambaa faslaa taey kar chukay hain	to have crossed a long distance of time
samay samay per	from time to time
aeyk aeyk kar kay	once by once (one by one)
baaree baaree say	turn by turn
[no collocations for beginning or end of time]	
waqt khatam; samay samaapt	end of time (not a collocation)

II. An orbital/circular course

There are, likewise, few phrases that predicate of time an orbital course.

zindagi aeyk chakkar haey	life is a circle (not a collocation)
zindagi ghoom phir kar phir waheen	life roams around and comes back to the same place again (not a collocation)
waqt/samay phir aayegaa	time will come again
baar baarambaar	again and again
zindagi kee chaal	the walk of life

III. Space-time deixis

Jo mayray saamnay *haey us tak main pahoonch jaaoongaa.*
What lies *before* me (in space/time) I shall reach.

Jo ho chukaa, woh mayray peechay *rah gaya.*
What has happened/done is *behind* me (in space/time).

Jo kuch baad main *hogaa/aayegaa, woh mayray* peechay *rahayga*
(Hindi-Urdu).
Whatever happens/comes *in the after* shall follow me/will keep *behind* me.

(This collocation implies time as a schedule of events already laid out, as in "those who have gone before in time are ahead of me, those who follow me in time are behind me.")

Jo kuch baad main *hogaa/aayegaa, main us tak pahoonch jaaoongaa.*
Whatever comes *later/afterward* I shall reach.

Y *kay baad* X (Hindi-Urdu)	X follows Y in time

(The phrase is commonly used in cases when one needs to say "X happened after Y" or "X came after Y.")

Y *kay paeyhlay* X (Hindi-Urdu)	X precedes Y in time/X comes beforeY
abhee aur iss-hee waqt (Hindi-Urdu)	here and this very time
yaheen aur abhee (Hindi-Urdu)	here and now
paeyhlae (Hindi-Urdu)	before/earlier (in time)
iskay poorva (Hindi)	this before
hamaaray saamnay (Hindi-Urdu)	*in front of us* (in space)
peechay *rah jaana* (Hindi-Urdu)	*behind* in time/space
samay say aagay (Hindi-Urdu)	ahead of/before (in time)
samay/waqt say payhlay	*before* time
dauraan (Hindi-Urdu)	during
beech (Hindi)	between (time/space)
wahin aur usee waqt (Hindi-Urdu)	there and at that very time
baad main (Hindi-Urdu)	after (in time)
pashchaat (Hindi)	after (in time)

List E. Time is its method of ascertainment/measurement

ghadee	moment/point in clock time
aarambh main (Hindi)	in the beginning (of any event/ period)
shuru main (Hindi-Urdu)	in the beginning (of any event/ period)
samay/waqt kaa andaazaa lenaa	to estimate the time
vaha ghad'ee nikat aa rahee haey jab	that clock is drawing near when
ghad'ee aa rahee haey	that moment is drawing near when
waqt/samay kaa andaazaa rakhnaa	keep tabs on time (while doing X)
samay/waqt kaa dhyaan rakhnaa	keep track of time in/on one's mind*
waqt/samay kee gatee/taeyzee ko kam kar daynaa	reduce the pace of time
waqt/samay kee chaal dheemee kar daynaa	slow down the pace of time
samay/waqt say chalnaa	to move on (clock) time
samay/waqt say jaanaa	to go on (clock) time
jaanay ka waqt aa gaya	the time to go/leave has come
jaanay ka waqt	departure time (e.g., from life)
samay/waqt samaapt/khatam huaa	time has ended
waqt ka intayzar	to await a certain time

TIME IN SESOTHO

Below are more than 150 temporal collocations in Sesotho, collected and presented in the same manner as has been done for Mandarin and Hindi. The spelling is that devised for southern Sotho in government primary and secondary schools in the Republic of South Africa.

List A. Time is a partible entity

selebisa nako	cause time to be used
fetisa nako	cause time to pass

qeta nako	finish time
arola nako	separate (out) time
arorela nako	distribute/apportion (one's) time amongst
nka nako	seize/take time
hapa nako	snatch time
t'soara nako	catch, get hold of time
fuparela nako	grasp time
nako ea monetla	narrow time/moment/hour/ season
tsenyehelo nako	despoiling, harming, damaging of time
senya nako	spoil, damage, harm time
baballa nako	to take care of, husband time
boloka nako	save, keep, put by time
ba lenako	to be with (i.e., have) time
fa nako	give time
etsa lenane la nako	to put in a temporal order
morero oa (t'sebeliso ea) nako	plan for the use (outlay) of time
nako ke leruo	time is cattle (riches)
nako ke bohlokoa	time is preciousness
mphe/fana ka nako	be generous in giving one's time
ho ba mafololo ka nako	to be quick and eager with (one's) time
nako tse ntle	beautiful time (as period or occasion)
nako tse monyaka	time of pleasure, joy
nako tsa chai	time of good harvest
nako tse monate	time of sweet(ness) (i.e., tasting food)
nako tse mpe	evil, wicked time(s)
nako tsa lerole	period/season of dust storms
nako tsa tlala	period/season of hunger
nako tsa komello	period/season of drought
nako tsa mat'soenyeho	time of tribulation/oppression
nako tsa lifaqane	time of great calamities
nako tsa lintoa	time of war (warring)
nako tsa maqhutsu	time of disturbance/ disequilibrium

bala nako	to name the time (nowadays to read/count the clock time)*
nako e ngata	time that is plenty/ample
nako e senyegenyege	time that is a swarm (frantic)
qubu oa nako	time that is a heap (accumulation)
nako ea ho etsa/pheta X	time to do/accomplish X
nako ea ho etsahatsa X	time (in which) to cause X to happen
nako e itseng	time that is specifically existent (i.e., some time)
roba monakeli	casually to pass/to while away the time
tila tila	pass the time (dillydally)
mehlong ea	historical time (era) of
nakong tsa	(historical) age of
nako e nyane	time is small
hakaneha nako	forget time
ho se tsotelle nako	to not ignore time
ho se ipapise le nako	to not flout (i.e., conform oneself with) time
ho se khathalle nako	to lack courage for (facing) time
ho se be hloko ka nako	to not be inattentive to, uncaring of time
ka nako e hlakileng	with time that is bright/visible (i.e., in good time)
ho sa na lenako	to be with (have) time
motsotsoana	a bit of time
nakwoana	a bit of time
loant'sa nako	to fight time
kakatana le nako	to bear time as a heavy burden on the head supported with both hands
ho ea ho ile	the gone that goes (eternity)
chai e ka moso	the harvest is tomorrow (later/ in the future)*
monono o ka moso	fatness (of animals—i.e., riches/ reward is tomorrow—i.e., in the future)

monono oa ka moso o oa khaphatseha	the riches of tomorrow overflow
nako e felile	time is finished (used up)
ha ho sana nako	there is no time (there)
t'soara nako	hold onto time

List B. Time is its effects

nako tse thabileng	time that gladdens*
nako ke ntat'a tsohle	time is the father of all (things)
nako ke mookameli	time is the dominating one
nako ke sesinyi	time is a destroyer
nako ke sebatalatsi	time is a leveler
lesupi la nako	ravages of time
re it'soarelelitse ho nako	we hold onto ourselves by (means of) time
re it'setlehile ka nako	we lean ourselves against time
nako e ea honyolla	time draws (pulls) out (things)
nako e bea pont'seng	time puts things in full (public) view
nako e ea hlahisa	time causes (things) to happen
nako e ea apola	time uncovers (i.e., discloses)
nako e ea upolla	time unearths (i.e., discloses)
nako e ea utolla	time uproots (i.e., discloses)
nako e ea rarolla	time untangles (i.e., makes clear)
khakhathiloe ke linako	to be beaten repeatedly by time
ruthuthiloe ke linako	to be wrestled by time
nako e ea ikela	time makes things go away
nako e fenya tsohle	time defeats everything
nako mohale oa bahale	time is the bravest of the brave
ha ho se ke emang ka pele ho nako	there is nothing that can stand before (i.e., cause to stop) time
nako ke makhona tsohle	time is the enabler of everything
nako le lietsahala li a o oela/kuka	time's happenings befall one/ engage one
ha ho eo nako e mo emelang	there is no time that waits for one
nako e ea ipusa	time rules itself

ha se lehlahana la mang kapa mang   (time) is not one subordinate to
                                              anyone

List C. Time is a medium in motion

nako ha entse e ya	as time was going on
nako e t'soanetseng ha e fihla	as the necessary time arrives
nako e fihlile	the time/moment has arrived
ha nako e ntse e ea	as the time was passing/going
ha nako e feta	as time passed
ho tsamaea ha nako	the going/marching of time
ho lelemetshea ha nako	the flow of time
ho nyolosa le ho theosa ha nako	the rise and ebb of time
ho ya ha nako	the goings of time
nako e ea tla e	the time is coming when
nako e tseleng e	time, which is on the way (here), when
nako e tlilo fihla e	(the) time will arrive when
nako e mphitile ke ntse ke ahlame	time passed me by (I still gaping)
nako e mpotile ka thoko	time went around me to the side*
nako e ea tsamaea	time is going/marching on
nako e ea ikela	time is going on on its own
nako e ea ea	time keeps on going
nako e nka mehato	time trods on
nako e ea thella/e feta	time slips/glides (by)
nako e ea tla	(the) time is coming
nako e shebile koano	time is facing this way
nako e haufi	(the) time is near
nako ea atamela	time is approaching
nako ke eo e se etla fihla	it is time that is about to arrive
emisa nako	to stop (work) of time
t'soara nako e re khekhenene	grasp and hold time still
mehlala ea nako	the footprints/tracks of time*
ho ba nakong	to be with on the time (of the occasion)

ho matha ka nako	to run with (i.e., "on") time (in general)
ho mathela nakong	to run on time (i.e., on a specific schedule)
ha ho eo nako e mo emelang	there is no one for whom time stands/stops
nako e potlaketse pele	time hastens forward
nako e habile pele	time moves quickly forward
nako e mathela pele	time runs forward
e be e sale entse e ea nako	time is always going
nako ea fofa	time flies
nako e be sale e it'supa pele	time is always directing itself forward
nako ea ema khekhene	time stops still (standing)
nako e lesisitheho	time dawdles/drags on stubbornly

List D. Time is a course

I. A linear course

nako e khut'soane	time is short
hloelisa nako tse tlang	to look from above at time that comes
sheba tse tlang	to look ahead to those things coming
sheba bokamoso	to look at things of tomorrow
sheba tse fetileng	to look at the things that have passed
sheba tsa maloba	to look at the things of yesterday
ha sesa feleng	that place that does not give out (infinity)
ile boilatsatsi	gone to the place of no day/sun (infinity)
qalo ea nako	beginning of a period of time/ age/era
nako e telele	a long time

ho ea ho ile	to go and go (on and on)*
ho tsamaea le linako	to go along with the times
methati ea nako	ridges (course) of time
bolele ba nako	length of time
nako e kana	time of this length
ka pele ho nako	in front of (ahead of) time (as a schedule)
ho nea nako mokokotlo	to give one's back to time (be ahead of time)*
e ea morao nakong	go back into an earlier period of time
hloela tse ileng	look at from above that which is gone (in time)
mehlaleng ea nako	paths of time
maqhubung a nako	on the waves (i.e., wandering course) of time
ka motsotswoana o nepahetseng	just the right moment (lit. "on target")
ka ho panya ha leihlo	in the blink of an eye (the "nick" of time)
ka morao ho nako	behind/after time
ka nako(ng)	with the time (of an occasion/event)
le nako	with (accompanying) time
ho hatela pele ho meso	to proceed forward toward the dawn
nako e a noaboloha	time stretches lethargically because nothing is happening

II. An orbital/circular course

(There are no collocations in this category; the expressions below are ordinary sentences.)

nako e (li) ea potoloha	time revolves (i.e., events recur)
nako li it'supa moliqalileng teng	time points (directs) itself to where it started

III. Space-time deixis

X *e latela* Y	X it follows Y (space and time)
X *e tla ka morao ho* Y	X it comes at the back of (behind, later) Y (space and time)
X *tsamaea mehlaleng ea* Y	X goes in the tracks (i.e., footprints) of Y (space and time)
X *e etella* Y	X precedes/leads Y
X *e tla pele ho* Y	X (is seen by an observer) to come in front of (before) Y
X *e ka pele ho* Y	X is (absolutely) at/with/to the front of Y (space and time)
mona hang hang	right here here (here and now)
hang ka motsotso oono	here with that moment (then and there)
tse ka pele ke tla fihla ho tsona	those things in front (of me), I will come to them (space and time)
tse tlang ke tla tla ho tsona	those things that come, I will come to them (space and time)
tse seng li etsahetse ke lifuraletse	those (events) that have already happened, I turn away from (i.e., to leave behind)
tse tlang/fihlang ha 'mamorao, li tla nlatela	those things that come/arrive behind/later, they will follow me
tse ileng tsa etsahala pele/pejana, tsa ke li siile morao	things that have happened before/earlier, I have left them behind
se leng ka pele se sa tlilo estahala	that which is in front has not come to happen
se leng ka pele se ha'mamoraona	that which is in front is later
se sa tla fihla re shebana le sona	that which has not yet arrived/happened, we face

List E. Time is its method of ascertainment/measurement

lahleheloa ke nako	to be lost by time (lose time)*
fetoa ke nako	to be passed by time*
bolela nako	tell one the time
bala nako	read/count the time (contemporary usage)*
fetisa nako	make time pass*
liehisa nako	to cause time to be delayed*
ka nako e baliloeng	at the time agreed upon
lekanya nako	to weigh/compare/heft the time

Each collocation in each of these four languages could, of course, be translated into a well-formed phrase in any other language. This is not at issue here, nor is this idea any longer very controversial. But this investigation of the spatialization hypothesis raises different questions—namely, (1) Which of those collocations occurring in any one language are found *as collocations* in any and all other languages, irrespective of the culture(s) of any given language's native-speaking population(s)? (2) Which collocations are unique to a particular language because they express demonstrable, culturally particular background conditions of belief and institutionalized language use?

We see here collocational evidence from four languages/cultures which reveals how metaphorically "time" is schematized in language and therefore, I argue, how #time# is experienced. There appear on the face of it in these data five basic metaphorically constituted experiences that are predicated of time. Now, as we took some pains to explain in Chapter Four, this does not mean that time is strictly included in these categorizations. This is not a taxonomy of time. Rather, something inchoate—expressed, for example, by "time," "shi," "samay/waqt," or "nako"—has been the argument that such predicates as entity, effect, linear course, orbital course, medium in motion, method of ascertainment, and deictic space syncategorematically have typified. In this process, both "time" and its predicates are changed by the metaphoric interaction. So #time# is not, for example, *simpliciter* a channel dug in the ground, a line connecting points in space, an orbiting body or an orbit itself, or a tangible entity. "Entity," "effect," "course," "medium," "motion," and so on are names for new intentional categories when they are metaphorically predicated of "time."

Even if one cannot finally and determinately state what #time# is, these collocations show that, across languages and cultures, the same predicates have been used in the same collocational structures to predicate something—often the same thing—of "time." And if (1) "time" is what is said of it, (2) if it is how it is described, and (3) if statements and descriptions in language are the expression of experience, we can say that #time# has been similarly experienced in diverse settings and places.

Let's see if this is borne out in further analysis of the linguistic and cultural evidence.

CHAPTER SIX

#Time# and "Time": Analysis of Data

To draw valid conclusions from this study, we must establish that the cultural backgrounds of the communities from which the data are drawn represent, for all practical purposes, all the cultural variation or variety that is theoretically interesting or necessary to consider in addressing the questions posed. We do not want to draw spurious conclusions of collocational universality because cultures of two or more languages' native speakers happen by chance, diffusion, borrowing, conquest, or colonization to share similarities that might issue in similarities of collocational expression. To the extent that similarities or commonalities of collocation are found among these four languages, these must subsist despite the supervenience of marked cultural differences in beliefs or institutional structure that inform respective experiences of #time# or "time."

Further, we need to have enough understanding of the culturally particular background of the respective speech communities that we can safely infer just why given nonuniversal collocations are distributed the way they are over a distinct subset of languages. We seek a basis for claiming that language-unique collocations occur precisely because of culturally particular ideological or institutional conditions.

#TIME# AND "TIME" IN THE WEST

A moment's reflection makes clear that we in the West organize our everyday lives around mechanically calibrated time composed of exact and equivalent durations between successive (clock) events that are indifferent to all possible meaning or significance. The essence of clocks in our culture is uniform motion or other transformations of state. Only in virtue of such a conception and physical manifestation can time be experienced (1) as conceivably isotropic (reversible) but practically anisotropic (nonreversible) and (2) as independent of all other events, occasions, activities, purposes. A mechanical, clock-based ideology of time goes back at least to the thirteenth century, and much earlier than that if we include sundials, water clocks, hourglasses, and other devices for metricating intervals between planetary or solar "clock" events. As Frake (1985) has shown in his studies of maritime navigation, pre–mechanical-clock medieval Europe was very interested in the clock function—that is, measuring time—even if, because of the lack of cadastrally set mechanical clocks, they could not develop a standard time.

Such manifestation of time becomes part of a shared, normative order when (1) clocks are placed in centers of power and control—public monuments, cathedrals, courts, factories, and universities; (2) all production and other activity is coordinated by authoritative or customary usages and decrees that are themselves predicated on "clock time"; (3) philosophers or theologians begin critically, publically to think about clock motion or other transformation in terms of formal systems (e.g., myths or mathematics) and to use such knowledge as part of theodicies or "natural" explanations; and (4) people's everyday lives grow to conform with time's culturally fetishized metrications (see Braudel 1984; Hobsbawm 1984; or Worsley 1984 for discussion of the commodification and public regimentation by clock time beginning in the Middle Ages with the rise of capitalism).

Under circumstances such as these, *time becomes the clock*—a development which is neither "natural" nor taken for granted. To wit:

> Who in this place set up a sun dial to cut and hack my days so wretchedly into small pieces. When I was a small boy my belly was my sun-dial. (Plautus in Rome, 254 B.C.)

> In town, your life is divided up by the number-pointer [clock]. You do nothing by desire or by circumstance or by custom, but rather only by the number-pointer. (Segatlhe in Kgaphamadi, Botswana, A.D. 1974)

Plautus and Segatlhe each experienced the beginning of a world according to mechanical or artifactual clocks, a world whose evolution is recorded in language use.

Many historians have noted how in the history of the West the (mechanical) clock came to exemplify not just time but our culture's conception of the universe itself—"the clockwork universe." For five hundred years, 1300–1800, the clock was the premier organizing metaphor for ontologic claims of physical order and the justification of claims for creation by God (the "Watchmaker God") as well (Macey 1980:65–122). This is perhaps the ultimate in the culturally peculiar fetishization of time, which, in a world of clocks, loses all sense of occasion, all sense of place-time, period (age), or happening. Before a day had become merely twenty-four hours, it was a god's occasion. We have lost words like *betide*, which meant period-of-happening-in-a-place. (*Tide* is an older form of *time*. "Woe betide" and "glad tidings" are survivals of this.)

Traditions of #time# and "time" go back much further than the Middle Ages. The Homeric Greeks had two profound temporal notions in their cosmologies: time is (1) a medium moving (2) in an orbital course. In much of Greek thought of both the Great and Little traditions, time is circular. The circular orbit is the exemplum of uniformity—apparent motion without structural change. Time is events going through a cycle, round, or turn—in particular, ontogenetic cycles of growth, achievement of a critical moment (*kairos*), decay, destruction, and renewal—which begins and ends at an origin point from which events begin again. Time is the never-beginning, never-ending succession of a finite number of events and affairs, which repeat themselves endlessly. So time is everlasting; it has no beginning and no end. Eternity—timelessness—applies both to the earlier and later. While there is history, it is sinusoidal, repeating itself in cycles of unknown amplitude or frequency. Such a view of time is intimately bound up with propitiousness, fate, and destiny (*kairos*)—appropriate, foretold, foreordained place-time for certain events which are the ultimate judgment or consequence of our acts. (For a cogent and concise discussion of the textual sources of my brief characterization, see G.E.R. Lloyd 1976.)

The Greek word *chronos* ("time" in some senses) does not occur frequently in early Greek literature (e.g., Homer), and it in no way expresses the range of senses of modern English "time." For example, in the *Iliad* and *Odyssey*, it occurs but nine times and means in each occasion "a period of duration." The vocabulary of early Greek temporal experience is expressed by specific events and occasions as day, night, year, month, "hour," periodic activity. The temporal experience predicated of these events very often involves the notions of "completion of plan or purpose" (*telos*) and "coming around"/"coming back"/"turning around" (*peri-telos*).

In Homer's day (ca. 800 B.C.), temporality was experienced as durations between successive events—the concreteness of the before-and-after in endless cycles. But by 500 B.C., the Greeks had, in synergy with cultural developments in Asia, established places and positions dedicated to critical or philosophic thought. Beginning perhaps with Pythagoras, the concrete, before-and-after, event-bound, cycling conceptions of temporality were appropriated as objects of formal critical thought. #Time# as an ideal conscious construction was born. The Greeks never shed completely the Homeric folk tradition of temporality but appropriated its contours in a variety of often contradictory ways as basic data for formal philosophic investigation (see Fraser 1987 for a very readable summary).

The ancient Middle East comprised other cultures that have contributed to Western cosmologic tradition. An ofttimes nomadic, wandering, or refugee people, the ancient Hebrews saw their identity as predicated not on space or place but on faithful reproduction and recruitment from procreation. The "People" remain integral by generation from generation to generation. This process had a beginning in a covenant—a Word—which included the creation of time. The Word, in continuing, makes time from generation to generation until the covenant is fulfilled. So time, being created, has a beginning and an end. It is bounded by God's Word to his (Chosen) People. Time is manifest in the events of God's design. Time reveals, discloses, unfolds the Word—that is, the succession of events between the Creation and the Salvation. While Creation is temporally determinate, Salvation (the end of time) is not. Time in this cosmology is history; history is the Word; and history, which the Word narrates, is linear, unique, finite, and teleological. God is not, however, coterminous with the Word, Creation, history, or time but is, rather, their author. (For an exegetical expansion of my summation, see Neher 1976.)

The Christians in Rome adopted much of Hebrew cosmology but added their own urgency to the agenda of Salvation. Christianity made Salvation an imminent aspect of time. They believed the time (of judgment) was at hand. With the "second coming," time would end—that is, there would commence the time of Eternity where everything was set. The key to getting there lay in conversion—which was to change one's ways and follow the Way, as Saul did on the road to Damascus. Time is a path, a way, a course that leads (via Salvation) from the Creation to Eternity. This path or way is a definite sequence of epochs, ages, or periods, which are the content of God's plan for people and constitute the history of the process of Salvation. But God intervenes timeously (e.g., the birth of Christ) to make—or at least to mold—these epochs in consideration of human initiatives. They are not foreordained. For Christianity (in Rome), time is history, which is the linear, nonrepeatable, progressive, finite, teleological succession of events beginning with Creation and ending in Eternity. Concordances of the New Testament usually describe "time," either directly or obliquely, as a path, way, or course (see Pattaro 1976 for comment on New Testament textual material).

This sketch of Western cosmologic notions might suggest that many English collocations derive from and express key aspects of Greek, Semitic, Christian (Roman), and medieval cosmology. Greeks certainly conceived of time as a moving medium, which always and eternally turns, coming around, in a circular course, inexorable and teleological. Segments, durations, or periods of this time were understood to be appropriate or propitious for certain events and occasions—hence the notions of a right or proper time. Early Hebrews and Christians conceived of time as unique and linear, where periodization was based on divine acts (e.g., Creation, Salvation, Eternity), yet where time could also be empty of prescribed content—a course in which events move.

However appealing may be the idea that all time collocations in English derive from culturally contingent experience in the West, we cannot justify this without cross-cultural, cross-language investigation. Indeed, as we shall see, there are very good reasons to reject or substantially revise such a conclusion.

#TIME# AND "TIME" IN CHINA

In the tradition and history of any civilization, many accretions to its ideologies will take place. Such accretions are never fully systematized and are rarely even collected or assembled. Rather, they exist as more or less distinct, yet interacting, provinces of meaning, often maintained by different groups, classes, schools, regions, occupations, and so on. We saw this clearly in our brief discussion of Western temporal ideologies, and it is equally true for China.

Much early Chinese philosophy postulated abstract conceptions of an absolute or relativistic space-time. "Time and its content were often the subjects of discussion and speculation in the philosophical schools of the Warring States Period (ca. 4th century B.C.). . . . [In a text of about 120 B.C. we read,] all the time that has passed from antiquity until now is called *chou*; all the space in every direction, above and below, is called *yü*. The Tao (the Order of the Universe) is within them" (Needham 1965:1). In Needham's view, *yü-chou* has the essential meaning of "space-time."

In the book of Mo Tzu (ca. 400 B.C.) and in derivative later works, we find stipulative definitions given to terms that appear frequently in our list of collocations. Thus, *chiu* [*jiu*] (duration) includes all particular *shih* [*shi*] (time-occasions). "When an object is moving in space we cannot say . . . whether it is coming nearer or going farther away. The reason is given under *fu* (spreading or setting up coordinates). . . . Talking about space, one cannot have in mind only some special district (*chhü*). It is merely that the first step of a pacer is nearer and his later steps farther away. The idea of space is like that of duration. . . . Time and space are alike, without boundaries" (Needham 1965:2–3).

In Needham's view, Mohist thought on time came very close to that of the Greeks of the same period in developing the notion of the functional dependency of motion on a time coordinate, even though the Mohists lacked a deductive geometry. However, it was not Mohist but Taoist/Confucian thought that gained hold as the de rigueur folk model of time. As Needham states: "The *philosophia perennis* of Chinese culture was an organic naturalism which invariably accepted the reality and importance of time. . . . Subjective conceptions of time were . . . uncharacteristic of Chinese thought. . . . Time itself remained inescapably real for the Chinese mind. This contrasts strongly with the general ethos of Indian civilization and aligns China with the inhabitants of that other area of temperate climate at the Western End of the Old World" (1965:ix).

The Confucians rejected the realist and idealist conceptions of infinite absolute time or time relative to a coordinate system. For them, always preoccupied with human affairs,

> time entered into their considerations only in relation to the appropriate times . . . for action. The mean or norm *(chung)* was the guide for emotion and action, but it must be flexible in application, for circumstances alter cases. . . . Hence it is a timely mean *(shih chung)* that one must follow. . . . [According to Feng Yu-Lan, this notion is akin to the Greek *idios kairos* mentioned above—the appropriate, propitious, decisive moment for action.] In the *I Ching*. . . this conception of the right timeliness in everything is very prominent. (Needham 1965:5–6)

The neo-Confucian school of the eleventh to thirteenth centuries A.D. drew eclectically on ideas from Mohism, Taoism, Buddhism, and Confucianism in formulating philosophies of time. Their ideas, especially those of Taoist origin, are expressed in the collocations presented above as cycles of recurrence and the importance of destiny *(ming)* within a cycle. According to Needham,

> nothing could be more striking [in neo-Confucian thought] than the [Taoist] appreciation of cyclical change. . . . Returning is a characteristic movement of the Tao. . . . Indeed, time *(shih)* is itself generated . . . by this uncreated and spontaneous never ceasing circulation *(yün)*. The whole of nature *(thien)* could be analogized with the life cycles of living organisms. [A right, propitious, appropriate time for every-

thing is seen on analogy with morphologic changes in organic onto-genesis.] This was the meaning of destiny *(ming)*, hence the expressions *shih-yün* and *shih-ming*. (1965:6)

Needham suggests, following Granet (*La pensée chinoise*, 1934), that the cycles of Chinese time were separated from one another in discrete units.

> Granet concluded that time in ancient Chinese conception was always divided into separate spans, stretches or blocks. . . . "The Chinese preferred to see in time an ensemble of eras, seasons, and epochs. Time and space were never conceived apart from concrete actions. . . . The Chinese decomposed time into periods just as they decomposed all space into regions. The Chinese never bothered about imagining time and space as homogeneous matrices suitable for housing abstract concepts." (Quoted in Needham 1965:7)

> "*Shih*" always seemed to imply specific circumstances, specific duties, and opportunities; it was essentially discontinuous, "packaged" time. . . . For the ancient Chinese time was not an abstract parameter, a succession of homogeneous moments, but was divided into concrete, separate seasons and their subdivisions. The idea of succession as such was subordinated to that of alternation and interdependence. (Needham 1965:7–8)

Needham rightly notes that this is not the whole view, as Chinese astronomy was not totally wedded to "boxed" time, nor was Chinese horology. Nevertheless, there is a powerful current of "occasionalism" in all Chinese thought on time. That is, moments of time are significant because of what they portend, prefigure, or make possible. Time is not empty but marks—indeed, constitutes—significant events, opportunities, tendencies in the real natural world. Telling time in China means reading the signs of the time as much as it means discerning abstract clock events. Even in Chinese horological philosophy, the notion of time retains significance beyond clock events. Thus *tshun chin nan mai tshun kuang yin* [*cunjin nanmai cunguangyin*] (an inch of gold will not buy an inch light-dark [time]) or *chhih pi fei pao tshun yin shih ching* [*chibi feibao cunyin shijing*] (a foot of jade is no treasure but struggle for an inch of light-dark [time]) (quoted in Needham 1965:17. Pinyin supplied by author).

Larre holds concordant views:

Shih refers to time in general indicating qualitative duration. The state of consciousness, as duration, whether permanent or successive is *shih*. . . . Time is relevant to human activity. . . . *Shih* involves the idea of situation, of a combination of circumstances which, if favourable, constitutes an opportunity to do something. Used as a verb, *shih* means to adapt oneself to circumstances, to come at the right moment, to fuse with a particular state of affairs, to be in harmony with things at the moment. (Larre 1976:36–37)

In sum, Chinese philosophic elaboration of "time" is accomplished in terms of (1) the space and movement or unfolding of nature's events, (2) the "fit" between human actions and nature (propitiousness/auspiciousness), and (3) the space-time conjunction of human and natural actions (proper or precious occasion). Telling time in China was—and to some degree, I am led to believe, still is—as much a matter of divining or discerning the energies, forces, tendencies, proclivities of the moment as it is computing clock events per se. In this sense, the Chinese see time as a real, natural duration/situation/occasion with qualitative value that cannot be separated from the clock events that mark it. As we in the West require matter and motion-as-quantity for time, the Chinese require for it the quality of events and purposes.

#TIME# AND "TIME": SOME COMPARISONS OF ENGLISH AND MANDARIN

Our sampling of collocations provides ample evidence that specific aspects or properties of Taoist/Confucian thought appear in modern Mandarin in the form of collocational patterning. The collocational privileges of occurrence of the central notion, *shi*, index this directly—thus *shishi* (time-condition), *shiyun* (time-fate), *liangshi jiri* (good, auspicious day), *chengshi* (seize the favorable moment), *shilai yunzhuan* (time come, fortune turn), *shiyun buji* (the times are not propitious), *shiguo fengyi* (time passed, wind changed), *shijian* (section, "box" of time), *shihou* (season/stage/moment in cycle).

Likewise, many collocations in English express an original experience of temporality in our culture, as it has become organized around clocks over the past twenty-five hundred years. For example, we see phrases that express the experience of

1. The burning of notched sticks or knotted rope: "time to burn," "mark time"
2. The flow of water in *clepshydra* (water clocks) or sand in an hourglass: "lose time" (*aquam perdere*), "gain time" (*aquam dare*), "run out of time" (compare "the running of an hourglass"), "give time" (the refilling of the head of a *clepshydra*), "the sands of time," "flow of time" (*aqua labia*), "time has run down"
3. The motion of heavenly bodies as reflected on sundials or astrolabes: "time waxes and wanes," "time moves," "time returns" (apparent zodiacal movement), "long hours/days" (the shadow's length)
4. The motion both of dials/hands and the works of weight- or spring-driven ("mechanical") clocks: "time weighs heavy," "time/the hour is up" (hand position vertical—the "prick of noon" in Shakespeare's ribaldry), "set the clock back/ahead," "time is going," "speed up/slow down time"
5. Many phrases reflect the arbitrary power of clock events as measures of other events including other clock events (i.e., keeping ratios between their event intervals constant—in particular, keeping them synchronized—and comporting oneself and communal life with such clock events): "keep time" (those who coordinated clocks with solar/celestial phenomena were "timekeepers"), "mind time," "tell time" (originally "told" by runners/messengers who broadcast sundial readings; later done by bells [German *Glock* (bell) and English *clock* have the same origin]), "run on time" (compare "the running of an hourglass," not trains!), "early/late," "in/on time," "divide time," "tight schedule" (clock spring wound tight).

Our data for English seem to suggest that, with the establishment of clocks as the embodiment of time, it was not long before the experienced essence of clocks (uniform motion) became metonymically the experienced essence of time itself. Time became a medium in uniform motion. As space, with the advent of clocks, was seen to have real dimensionality (extension) independent of clock time, so clock time came to be seen as having real duration independent of space. The clock became not simply the measure of time but its canonic exemplification.

With the advent of money of account, capitalism, and commodity production beginning in the twelfth century, time became a force or means of production—a tangible entity or resource— and a fetishized commodity. Hence we came to spend, waste, save, outlay, spare, borrow, steal, allocate, apportion, and use, as well as measure, time, which increasingly entered production and exchange with a market value and an opportunity cost. As the ultimate goal of doing in our culture became having (privately possessing) things, it is not surprising that we came to make use of, do something with, kill, have plenty (too little, not enough, too much) of some amount of time.

Under the imperatives of capital accumulation (economic growth), production shifted, in the period 1100 to 1350, from use values based in households and manorial estates to mass production by "free labor" for often distant markets. Life became temporally regimented over increasingly large areas and large numbers of people, for whom arbitrary, publicly marked times to do certain things became a way of life—wake up, go to work, work, knock off, go home, eat, pray, sleep.

While the Chinese collocations (or, more precisely, our sample) lack the numerousness of expressions for many of our Western "accounting," "marketing," and clock-inspired production, labor, and leisure practices, and even though we for our part lack the Chinese regard for propitiousness or preciousness of occasion, the two lists of collocations, English and Mandarin, nonetheless express remarkably similar temporal experiences. Specifically, we see, first, a small number of words that show wide privileges of collocation to compose temporal expressions: *shi* (with the sun radical), *dai* (successor/substitute in cycle), *jian* (partition/interval), *xian* (see with eye/be there), *lai* (come), *jiu* (enduring), *guang* (light). *Shi* comes closest in its distributional occurrence to being equivalent to the English word *time* and is used in modern Mandarin to translate the broadly, abstractly, and vaguely specified notion "time."

Second, we see numerous instances of the five categories instantiated already by the English expressions: (1) time as a partible entity, (2) time as a causal agent with effects, (3) time as a medium in motion, (4) time as a linear and as a circular course, including a space-time deixis in which the experiencer and experienced events have an unopposed horizontal, back-front, and before-after relationship, and (5) time as its method of ascertainment.

In Mandarin, the time-as-course and space-time deixis shows an interesting contrast with English which is worth examining, as it provides further indication of those aspects of temporal spatialization which may be invariant across languages/cultures as opposed to those that may be contingent. Mandarin collocations of space-time deixis express an experiential perspective in which time is a medium in motion-bearing events (like English), but unlike English, the experiencer is always stationary in the medium, facing the direction of the past—that is, that which has passed—with his or her back to the future. The past is before one; the future is/comes from behind. Though infrequent, this "back-to-the-future" temporal orientation is not unique to Chinese. It is found in Latin (see Bettini 1991 for a thorough analysis) and in certain native languages of Latin America—for example, the Mayan language, Quiche.

The endless course of time flows from behind the speaker, passing him or her, moving forever before/in front of the speaker into the past. The future, coming from behind the experiencer, moves closer and closer to him or her and the present. Once the time medium cum events have passed by the experiencer, they become past events and are before or in front of the experiencer. Events have, like the experiencer, a front (further past) back/behind (more recent past/future) orientation. Note that in English events moving in time or the moving of the medium of time itself ceases after they "pass" the speaker. The past remains stationary, and the speaker moves, leaving it behind. In Mandarin, events that are before or have passed the experiencer themselves continue to move further and further away from the experiencer, who remains "now" but still in the ordinal sequence.

In Mandarin, the before (past)/behind (future) orientation applies to the relative temporal positioning of all events, irrespective of the perspective of the "now" of the experiencer. Future and past events alike show what one respondent calls a "sequencing" or "scheduling." Events don't so much "happen" in time as they are "positioned" or "situated" in time. Past and future events maintain their situated before/in front of (past, earlier)/behind (after, later) relationship irrespective of the experiencer. Said differently, the speaker remains in sequence among events, despite the "passage" of the medium time. Thus, for example, if A and B are events and A "will pass" or "has passed" before B, then, expectably, B comes "after" A, and, conversely, A comes before B. In Mandarin, A was, is, and always will be situated in front of (*yiqian*) B, and, conversely, B was, is, and always will be situated behind A. So the "day before yesterday," in Mandarin, is the "day in front of (*qian*) (yester)day"; the year before last year is the "year in front of (last) year." The "day after tomorrow" is, in Mandarin, the "after/behind/in back of (*hou*) day"; the year after next year, the "after/behind/in back of year."

Mandarin has a vertical (up-down) dimension in its space-time deixis expressed collocationally. (In English we have this dimension, but it is not expressed in collocationally rich fashion: despite "down through the ages," we don't have "up through the past"; the "Descent of Man" doesn't have as sequel or converse the "Ascent of Apes.") In Mandarin, upper (*shang*) [toward or from the past] and down (*xia*) [toward or from the future] constitute the genealogical metaphor of time par excellence.

English space-time deixis, although similar to that in Mandarin, shows some specific points of contrast. Our English deictic collocations exhibit an interesting paradigmatic pattern. First, there are two metaphors of time in English deixis: (1) time is a relatively still course in which events move, and (2) time is a medium in motion bearing events along with it. Second, there are two attitudes taken by the speaker: (1) the speaker is stationary facing the future, or (2) the speaker is moving toward the future. The four combinations are displayed in tabular form below. The cells (combinations of metaphor and speaker attitude) are labeled (a), (b), (c), and (d), which I use for convenience of reference in the discussion that follows (table 3).

Perspective (a) presumes time is a course in which events move temporally, toward a stationary experiencer, who "stands" in and faces the direction in the course from which events are coming. Collocational or other attestation for this includes Christmas is coming; who knows what the day will bring; tomorrow comes after today; the past is behind us. In this perspective, events approach, are next to one (now), pass, and finally have passed. Events in the future move toward one. But once they have passed, they cease to move. The past does not recede. Events are oriented so that they face toward the speaker. If X happens before Y, then X comes before (i.e., in front of) Y. When we move an appointment forward, we move it closer to the present—the speaker's now. If something is before (in front of) a speaker in space, one comes to it (later). If something precedes a speaker in time (when time is a course), then it is behind (to the back of) one (e.g., I've left my past behind).

In perspective (b) time is itself a medium in motion bearing a schedule or sequence of events with it toward the experiencer, who faces the "flow" of time. Collocational or other attestation of this perspective includes time is coming when, the future is upon us, time marches on, they have gone before us.

The contrasts between perspective (a) and (b) have definite effects in collocation or in "selection restriction" in structures of predication or modification. For example, the temporal adverb *soon* (comparative *sooner*) expresses a temporal relationship that requires perspective (a)—that the course of time be still and events or the speaker's experience of them moves in that course, either from the present to the future or from the future to the present. Further, *soon* expresses a temporal orientation from the experiential present toward the future (even when speaking of or in past time).

By contrast, the locative denominal adverb *early* (comparative *earlier*) expresses a temporal relationship within events that are themselves anchored to positions in the temporal medium. They move solely because the medium of time itself moves. One can't

Table 3

		Metaphor of Time	
		Time a Still Course	Time a Medium in Motion
	Stationary, Facing Future	(a)	(b)
Speaker's Attitude			
	Moving toward Future	(c)	(d)

say, for example, "*Easter came sooner last year than it did this year." But one can say, "Easter seemed to come sooner last year than it did this year." "Easter will come sooner this year than it did last year" suggests that the coming is experiential rather than calendric. "*Christmas came sooner than we thought" cannot imply that "Christmas came earlier than we thought." "Easter is coming early" implies that it occurs on an early time point in the moving temporal medium. "Easter is coming soon" implies that the experiencer is taken by how apparently fast Easter is moving in the stationary temporal course.

In (c) the individual himself moves along a course in which events are temporally situated. Here the individual comes to events. Events in the farther, more distant future are farther ahead; one comes to them later and later in time. One faces, goes into the future. One leaves the past behind. "Earlier" (the past of the event duration itself) maps onto back, behind in time. "Later" maps onto before or in front of one.

Only in perspective (c) can the past undergo relative temporal movement—by virtue of the experiencer's movement on into the future and away from the past. For example, "I'm leaving my childhood farther and farther behind." One cannot say, "*My childhood is getting farther and farther behind (me)." Yet one can say, "In my mind's eye/memory/consciousness, my past is receding." Here the gaze of one's mind's eye is the medium in which the past is an event receding. In perspectives (a) and (b), a person in the medium must be relatively stationary, facing the direction of the future. Perspective (d) seems to be a null set in English. Thus one cannot say collocationally, "The future and I are headed toward each other." Unlike the case of Greek, where the medium moved in endless circles and cycles of the before-and-after, for us the flow is linear, from the future toward the present and past one. But, curiously, the flow of time and all that it bears stops when the time passes the present, the "now" of the experiencer. The only way the past can "have" relative movement is to adopt the view that the experiencer herself moves on, leaving behind things of the past.

Although I cannot prove the point, it seems quite tenable that the elaboration and veneration of ancestry and heritage in China are concordant with the perspective that one faces the past, that one is situated in time and events, that the future is behind and down and the past is in front and up. Likewise, it seems quite unremarkable that in the West, where the past is to be overcome (it's even the source of sin itself!), where the future holds progress, improvement, a more perfect union, and even, say some, salvation and eternal life, we would face the future and await eagerly its arrival or journey to it. ("It's morning in America" and "America is Tomorrow's Land" are nice, albeit jingoistic, expressions of English space-time deixis.)

An important question that the Chinese and English collocations raise is whether their concordance and similarity arise, as Needham intimates, from the preoccupation in both cultures with engineering, with mechanical, solar, or celestial time reckoning, and with mass production, using highly organized human labor power. An obvious alternative hypothesis, flowing from aspects of the spatialization thesis, is that there exists a panhuman disposition, manifest in all languages and cultures, to construct time along certain rather invariant lines, presumably based on the transcultural template of "embodied" space and motion.

If the latter is the case, we would expect to find temporal collocations like those we have seen for English and for Mandarin in any language, spoken in any culture, irrespective of what cosmologic, philosophic, mythic, or other conscious notions of time have developed. This is not to say, of course, that temporal collocations would be confined to the kind we have seen. Indeed, we have already shown that temporal collocations will sediment and reflect culturally contingent experience, such as that manifested by the celebration of mechanical clocks or the future (Europe) or of ritual occasion, heritage, or the past (China).

To perform the critical experiment needed to select one hypothesis over the other, we require two linguistic/cultural settings: (1) a culture in which there is a venerable history of extensive, self-conscious, critical thinking about "time" but whose ideologies of time are radically different from those found in the cultures of Europe or China, and (2) a culture in which "time" has received little or no conscious attention or expression of any sort.

If temporal collocations in both such language/culture settings were to show significant overlap with those we have adduced for English and Mandarin, this would be strong evidence for a potent panhuman biocultural substratum for the concept "time." If the collocations were to show little overlap with those in English and Mandarin and seemed, in the first case, to be built around local cosmologic tenets and, in the second case, to be few in number or absent entirely, then we would have strong evidence for the purely contingent, culturally particular construction of "time."

Two languages/cultures that fulfill all the requirements for a critical test of this hypothesis are Hindi (Urdu) of North India and Sesotho/Setswana of southern Africa. To suggest how this is so, I must provide a brief description of relevant cultural features.

#TIME# AND "TIME" IN HINDI/URDU

In much Indian philosophy since Vedic times, "the existence of the universe—and hence the history of man and of the cosmos—comes under the sway of two superior forces: *kala* (time) and *karma* (the act). . . . The vision of time varies according to whether time is regarded as a power, the Self, or divinity. In a state of ignorance, time is the first thing to manifest itself, but in a state of wisdom, it disappears" (Panikkar 1976:63). Although in certain Vedic-inspired traditions, time "has no reality . . . except in the

moments in which divine or sacred acts [of sacrifice] are concerned," far more widely and currently held is the view that
"time is a cosmic power, . . . the fount and origin of reality. Time
is the creator of the creator, Prajapati, who is him/her/itself
Brahman, the principle of the universe" (Panikkar 1976:64–65). As
warrant for this heady idea, foreign to Westerners and Chinese
alike, consider the Vedic hymn:

> We see time, even though it is in many places at once
> Opposite all these existences.
> Time is also seated, they say, in the highest firmament.
> In oneness Time bore these existences,
> In oneness it encompassed them around.
> Time their father became time their son.
> No glory higher than this.
> Time engendered heaven above.
> Time also engendered the earths we see.
> Set in motion by Time, things which were
> And shall be are assigned their place.
> Time created Earth;
> In Time burns the Sun;
> In Time . . . the eye sees far-off existences.
> In time is consciousness; in Time,
> Breath; . . .
> In Time is sacred Fervour; in Time, yes, in Time
> Is concentrated the all-powerful Brahman.
> Time is the lord of all things,
> Time was the father of Prajapati.
>
> (quoted in Panikkar 1976:65)

"All reality depends on time, and even sacrifice . . . is likewise
subordinated to time. It is important to note the relationship . . .
between absolute time (the father) and empirical time (the son).
Here space is supported by and extended in time. Even inner
realities—consciousness and breath—are under the sway of time.
. . . *Kala* is here the supreme divinity" (Panikkar 1976:66).

> From time flow beings, through time they grow old, in time they are
> destroyed: time that is amorphous assumes shape. . . . Time ripens,
> time enfolds creatures. Time keeps watch when all are asleep. Time is
> hard to overcome. Time is the lord who works change in beings—that

which cannot be understood and that from which there is no return. Time is the destiny (*gati*) of everything. . . . [Time], that which is uniquely one, has many forms. . . . [It] controls every thing that exists. . . . Time is the cause of all; it is time that creates and destroys, that binds men by links and causes the joys and sufferings of men, regardless of their actions. . . . Time . . . hastens the progress of all beings toward dissolution. . . . Time is an ocean where one can see neither shore nor refuge. . . . Time being infinite caused the end; being without beginning creates the beginning, is immutable. (Panikkar 1976:66–67)

An Indian proverb (from the Veda) says, "Time cooks all things—indeed, is the great self. He who knows in what time is cooked he is the knower of the Veda."

In the four Vedas . . . we see our world as one in which creation and destruction pursue their relentless labor simultaneously. . . . As a defense against such a world, they advocate a belief in the insignificance of time's passage. Time, while real enough for daily chores, is judged unimportant in the economy of the universe. . . .

[In the Hindu conception] time negates time. The life of Brahma is 100 Brahma years, each of which has 360 Brahma days. During each Brahma day, Vishnu, the preserver and protector of the world, winks 1000 times. Each time his eyelids open, a universe appears and lasts for 12,000 divine years. As he closes his eyes, the universe vanishes. Each divine year consists of 360 human years. We get 155,520 trillion human years for one Brahma lifetime. [This is more than 10 billion times the estimated age of our universe to date!] When Vishnu's dream ends, the lotus closes and one Brahma lifetime ends. As Vishnu's dream resumes, the lotus once again opens and a new Brahma begins its [his] mission. (Fraser 1987:17–29)

In Indian conception, "time" is conceived statically rather than dynamically. . . . The substance of things is seen as basically unchanging. The Indian does not concede that we never step into the same river twice; he directs our attention, not to the flow of the water, but to the river itself, the unchanging universal. . . . Western people tend to comprehend action through its changing aspects, while Indians tend to consider that action is an unchanging aspect, even an attribute of existence. The persistent Indian conception of a transcendent [static] reality as more important than the phenomenal world it underlies and sustains results in a kind of individual sensitivity to time as the passage and flow of specific events. (Nakamura 1966:77–78)

In the Bhagavad-Gita, one of the foundational documents of Hinduism, the highest form of deity, in its destructive role, is . . . Time. This great poem, which probably dates from the third or fourth century B.C., in revealing the divinity as Time, that makes the worlds to perish, when ripe, and brings on them destruction, [invokes] a long-established tradition of Indian religious thought. . . . This implicit deification of Time would appear to have its roots far back in the Indian cultural past. (Brandon 1964:31)

The Hindu conception of time seems radically different from that which China or western Europe has presumed or produced. For many Chinese, time is a precious, tangible reality freighted with opportunity or portent. For many of western European/ North American background, time is a measurable reality that has a market value. Still, both in China and the West time has a successive before-and-after linearity to it. By contrast, it would seem from the accounts just cited that for many Indians empirical time is insignificant or is at most "the enemy" that destroys. Absolute time, *kaalavaada*, would seem to have ordered and ordained all things such that any struggle by human agency would in no way alter it. Indeed, the universe of empirical circumstance—past, present, future—in all space is contained in absolute time (divinity) itself.

"TIME" IN HINDI/URDU: DISCUSSION

In our collection of collocations in Hindi and Urdu, we find direct expression of almost all the tenets of Indian cosmology cited above. (Bear in mind that the language of these citations is Sanskrit, whereas our collocations are in contemporary Hindi and Urdu.) The causal omniscience of time is well represented: *waqt kay saamnay sab jhuktay hain* (everyone bows before time); *waqt say kya ladnaa* (why fight time?); *jab samay aataahai, tabhi woh cheez hoti haey* (when its time comes, only then does it happen); *wakt tabaah kartaa haey* (time ruins/wastes/levels/destroys); *samay naashak haey* (time is a destroyer); *samay sab khatam kar detaa haey* (time ends everything in destruction); *waqt kay saath sachchaayee saamnay aa jaatee haey* (time unfolds the truth); *waqt kay saamnay sab kee haar hoti haey* (time defeats all); *samay main utaar chadaav* (time raises and lets events fall). Two of my respondents stated that this list of stock expressions for the destructiveness and power of time could have gone on ad nauseam.

The absence of evidence is in no way evidence for the absence of a phenomenon. Still, there seem to be very few Hindi collocations that predicate of time a two-dimensional course, linear or orbital. There are no collocational counterparts in our Hindi sample for English collocations such as long time, short time, ahead in time, back in time, to progress in time, to move forward in time, to move back in time. Concordantly, there are no collocations in Hindi which are the counterparts to the English beginning of time or end of time. Further, there are no collocations for the circular orbiting of time itself. The expression *waqt phir aayegaa* (time will come again) is not a collocation and in any case means there "will be another occasion." While there are repetitions in life, conceived metaphorically as "round, circular, or orbital," this property of life is not collocationally predicated of time itself.

Some collocational expressions in Hindi for time ascertainment are influenced, of course, by mechanical clocks, as the reader can see. Interestingly, however, some collocations of time ascertainment in Hindi express an experience of "seeing," "casting one's vision or understanding" on characteristics of events (*aagay daykhnaa; bhavishya vichaarnaa; beetay samay par drishtee daalnaa*). In this sense, "telling time" in some Hindi expressions is akin to what we mean by "understanding the times."

We do not find many collocations, if any, in Hindi which predicate of time the many monetary, market, or commodity values that we have in English. And, despite the radically different ideologies of time which inform Indian experience, and despite having a linearly spatialized space/time deixis (which, as far as the data go, seems to be identical to that found in English) and ample experience of "linear" clock time, Hindi resists extrapolation of time as an indefinite line, either straight or orbital; thus *samay/waqt* do not collocate with scalar or vectoral metaphors of quantity.

But beyond these points of comparison and contrast, one thing seems quite clear—*the basic categories of collocational metaphors which we postulated for English and Chinese appear in Hindi as well.* True, the way the categories are metaphorically instantiated varies, and the variation in relative frequency of collocations among the categories is different, but these same five categories seem to partition the set of collocations for Hindi as effectively as they do in English and Mandarin. I say more about this in Chapter Seven.

A long history of scholarly philosophizing on and concern with the topic of "time" is one characteristic, at least, which the cultures and traditions of the West, of China, and of India share in common. Beginning about twenty-five hundred years ago in each of these cultures, the disparate folk knowledge contained in the then-existing oral traditions, or written transcriptions of these, from the preceding millennium became the subject of disciplined, critical thought by literate scholars of various schools, which had by this time become well established in the respective civilizations. Subsequently, aspects of these scholarly investigations were taken up as part of the larger folk knowledge or ideology that was, and still is, distributed—nonuniformly, of course—over the mass of the populations bearing these cultures. The result is that historically, as today, there has been a "time consciousness" that characterizes equally, but in different ways, the cultures of the West, of China, and of India. Among the three civilizations, this "time consciousness" has different properties, qualities, or characteristics because it is informed in part by quite different, culturally contingent scholarly thought and by folk thought as well.

Yet we have seen that, despite the differences in critical philosophy among the cultures examined, our five basic categories of temporal collocation appear and reappear persistently. Now in light of this one must raise the following issue: given sufficiently numerous, complex, and various traditions of scholarly philosophy about "time" within a culture's history, perhaps any civilization is going to stumble eventually onto just about all possible ways for a spatialized mind-set to think about something like #time#. If the culturally specific compilations of collocations here each represent two or three millennia's accumulation of thought on "time," then we might expect they would each eventually come to contain the same categories and content irrespective of the idiosyncracies of any particular culture's history.

Such a process could explain collocational universality by appeal to grades or levels of civilization and the convergence of content by static statistical sampling of *longue durée* historical events. Over time, lexicons would grow more alike, as ideas, discovered independently in different civilizations, accumulate and are sedimented collocationally. A purely cultural-historical explanation for commonality would be obvious and hence no reason to entertain the notion that basic categories of collocational expression represent *Bauplan* "default" values that any civilization will express, even if it overlays them with much culturally particular wisdom.

Fortunately, there is a way to test the competing claims of the two hypotheses: by study of temporal collocations found in a language spoken by people of a culture that has demonstrably no history or tradition of conscious, scholarly, philosophic thought that bears on the experience of #time# or on language use about "time." If we hypothesize that the numerousness and categorial structure of time collocations are a function of the cumulative processes of civilization, then a culture with no conscious philosophic notions of time ought to have no collocations that we might classify as "temporal"—or, at most, ones very different from those found in cultures with traditions of critical thought on the subject. If, on the other hand, the character and frequency of temporal collocations are deemed to arise from the human *Bauplan*, then we would expect temporal collocations with the same category structure in any language, no matter what its culture is like, including those that are ideologically indifferent to, or ignorant of, "time" as an object of critical philosophizing. A language and culture that meet all the conditions we require for a critical experiment to test the two competing hypotheses are found in Sesotho, a language and culture of southern Africa, whither we now repair.

#TIME# AND "TIME" IN SOUTHEASTERN AFRICA

Among Bantu-speaking Africans (about 150 million people today), there do not exist shared, conscious, propositionalized philosophies, cosmologies, mythologies, or other cultural constructions that we would recognize as being about "time" or other temporal experience. To be sure, there do exist notions—not, however, systematically organized or expressed—having what we would call temporal significance. Together, these create the contours of experience which can be subsumed within our metacultural category of "time." Ten years ago I set forth a portrait of these, which I here cite *in extenso*:

> Key to understanding specific hopes and fears among the Tswana is a knowledge of the cultural meanings which connect past and future in terms of Tswana apperception of time. . . . A pictorial representation will help me to present aspects of a traditional Tswana cosmogony as it was explained to me by various Tswana respondents [see fig. 2].

> What this pictorial metaphor highlights is the two-dimensional, and hence spatial, character of certain time experiences. To understand lived time [#time#], it must be realized that for the Tswana there is a coordination of . . . atemporal cosmologic time with progressive world time. The Tswana believe that there was a creation—a beginning of the cosmos (*tlholego*)—but much more importantly, that beginning continues throughout cosmologic time and is always present. It (*tlholego*) is an eternal existent. Existing time is orthogonal to cosmologic time and is infinite. Moreover, existing time has two aspects, both of which are given in the origins: world time and ancestral time. World time and ancestral time, while in complementary positions vis-à-vis the individual, parallel one another, each participating continuously in the origins of the cosmos. The basis for both the constant and the progressive in the nature of world events and ancestral time requires the conjoint role of cosmologic and existing time. The movement of the arrow along the axis of cosmologic time describes a path that takes one from the origin through life to death—that is to say, back to the origin. While the origin is atemporal and eternally present, existing time (world time and ancestral time) moves along the origin continually, sometimes close to it, sometimes far away.

> These two senses of time (existing time and cosmologic time) are required to understand Tswana lived time: age and aging. Age for the

PICTORIAL METAPHOR OF TSWANA
TIME-CONSCIOUSNESS

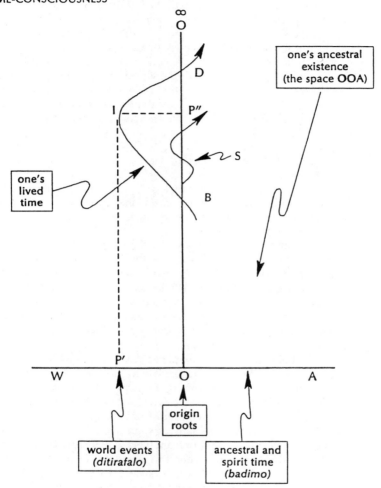

Figure 2. Pictorial metaphor of Tswana time consciousness. Past, present, and future are points in two-dimensional space. *Key to abbreviations:* O = Origin or root of Setswana; B = Birth of an individual; D = Death of an individual; S = Spirits; I = individual at given moment of existence = [P′, P″; O–O = cosmologic time (atemporal, eternal present); O–W = axis of world time; space of world time: OOW; O–A = axis of ancestral time; space of ancestral time: OOA; A–W = existing time, union of world and ancestral time.

Tswana cannot be the linear and homogeneous spatialized time of Newton applied to a biological definition of life. For that matter, most non-literate Tswana do not "know their age" if it is conceived in this way. For the Tswana, age has its most important basis in a set of social and ancestral relationships. Age is one's relation to a social order whose duration can only in part be conceived in terms of world time, for social order is only partly in the world of the living. Life in the world of the living is an aspect of life as a whole, not a period of time. The social order includes essentially the existence of the not-living, who, in virtue of being ancestors, are closest to the origins of the society and the people. Positive world time for the Tswana individual comprises a movement forward to a stage that is like the beginning. The conditions of the past—the ancestors, God, and their union—lie at the forwardmost extension of a person's anticipation of his/her being. The past of the world (*ditirafalo*) is unclear to the Tswana but will be clarified in the "time to come"—that is, when one is united with the ancestors who embody the final order established in the origins of Setswana.

In this context, a person's age can be conceived of in terms of nearness to the ancestors—closeness to the cultural root (*modi*) which ancestral existence embodies. Age also represents the accumulation of experience. Accumulation of experience recapitulates, to some degree, knowledge of the past—that end to which the future is headed. To put this metaphorically, for the Tswana, aging is a simultaneous movement in two directions away from a center: to a primordial past, which is the goal of the future, and to the end or goal of one's future, which is defined in terms of experience accumulated while alive. The Tswana believe children are quite close to the ancestors, to the final order which is also the beginning. Growth cuts one off from this "spiritual" closeness to the ancestors. But with continued growth into the time when one will become "a man of long ago," closeness to the ancestors is again increased. Many Tswana claim that the very young and the very old understand one another well, in part because they share knowledge based on closeness to the origins of Setswana. While a young child's knowledge of deep Setswana is accounted for in terms of his recent propinquity to the ancestors—children "come from" the ancestors—the old man is wise both because he is growing closer to the ancestors and because he has world knowledge or experience.

The Tswana concepts of age and time are not uniform. The interpreted meanings of these concepts change with age, as the individual constantly redefines and reconstitutes his/her own biography. Time is not an abstract, conceptual continuum which exists in virtue of linear relationships between distance and velocity. For the Tswana, time is composed of events. In virtue of this, living is an accumulation of time, not the passage of time, for living gives rise to wisdom and to the memory of experiences—the *sine qua non* of time. Because time is an aspect of events, the past is rich with experience and "deep in time." The future is shallow and, in imagination, rather impoverished. Its existence is composed largely of events normally extrapolated into the future. "Possibility" for the Tswana lies in the interpretation of the past, not in the imagining of an indeterminate future. . . .

These qualities of time intersect with the qualities of age in determinate ways. Aging is experiencing. Aging is "seeing with one's own eyes" (*boitebatebelo*). Influence in the community depends on the degree to which one has accumulated experience. Experience, to be of value, must be remembered; it must become a part of the self. In Setswana the idea of "advice" or "counsel" is closely linked to the concept of recalling prior experience. Knowledge for the Tswana is "remembering things past." The Tswana equate forgetting with lack of knowledge or ignorance. They say: "To have forgotten is similar to being puzzled." (Alverson 1978:166–72)

Robert Thornton's (1980) account of #time# and "time" for the Iraqw of Tanzania is similar in many respects to my account of the Tswana.

The chief characteristics of Iraqw narratives are (a) the lack of chronology; (b) the importance of oral performance and ritual; (c) the conservation of quality, place, and objects; and (d) the prominence of spatial relationships of events systematically related to one another in a topical way. Here we attempt to explore each of these aspects more fully.

In a formal, mathematical sense, topology is a geometry of space in which measurement of length, distance, angles, is not allowed. Measurement entails a standard of length or angle and an act of comparison by which this standard is applied to the whole space. Distances may be stated precisely with reference to the chosen standard and the act of comparison. The Iraqw do have a standard of [time] measurement. One may talk of years (*kuru*), months (*slahhangw*)—literally, "moons," days (*delo*), or hours (*loa*; literally, "suns," as in *loarmagá*, "What sun is it?" or "What time is it?"). They do not, however, use these standards of measurement comparatively to produce a general concept of uniform time, a chronology, that is, against which all

events may be compared. Years, months, days, and hours are parti-
tions of the flow of time, and, in the way we use the term here, are
topological. The creation of a uniform (e.g., Euclidian) space or a
uniform standard (e.g., a chronology) requires a logical act that the
Iraqw do not perform. Again, the experience of time is manifestly the
same, but the use of the concept is different. Among other peoples, a
genealogy of chiefs or a succession of generation sets [is an example]
of elementary chronology.

. . . I am making the distinction here between the topological
character of practical, sequential time and the linear, metric character
of chronology. In each case, there is a concept of a unit of time—a
discrete partition of temporality—such as the region of a chief or the
longevity of a generation. There is also the implicit logical act of
comparison between one reign and another, one generation and the
next, which posits an equivalence of units and uniform ordering of
units that derives from experience in the real world; namely, chiefs
beget chiefs, generations beget succeeding generations. Here we draw
the distinction between the partition of time and the act of ordering
these units into a uniform sequence (but not sequence itself) that can
serve as a general system of temporal reference. . . .

We must note the distinction between sequence and chronology.
Sequence is a physical and biological given. It is perceived in the
natural rhythms of the body and of the physical world. Chronology,
on the other hand, is a cultural, imposed order.

The Iraqw share with certain non-Western peoples a very limited
notion of change over time. This is not, I suspect, because they do not
perceive change in their circumstances or in the society. In informal
conversation, change is much discussed. . . . In formal discourse,
however, balance and repetition are emphasized. . . . The contrast
between the informal recognition of change and the formal denial of
any overall long-term change that does not repeat itself reveals a
contradiction between formal cultural ideology and individual experience. [I disagree with this interpretation that there is an ideological
contradiction here. The apparent paradox is resolved by postulating
two orders of time, cosmologic versus existent. See my discussion of
the Tswana above.] I was unable to discover any creation myth. For
the Iraqw, it seems, since the terms of existence are given today, they
always have been and always will be. . . . Similarly, there are no
stories that deal with the end of the world. There is little fascination
with the future. . . . There are no stories that deal with . . . the destiny
of man. Their goals are concrete . . . : to continue their expansion into
new lands and to preserve the territory they already occupy.

The lack of creation myths, the lack of teleological mythology, and the lack of a great deal of ceremony to mark the passing of the social person on his death are all consistent with the assumption that there is no real change in the things in the world, but merely a reordering. This concept is also consistent with the lack of time reckoning as a means of ordering thought about events in the past. . . . It is safe to say that there is no history among the Iraqw, if by "history" we mean the critical examination of narrative tradition about the past. (Thornton 1980:171–81)

Beidelman (1963) has reported, not dissimilarly, "time-reckoning" among the Kaguru of Tanzania, as has Bordieu (1963) for North African "peasants." Despite the apparent systematicness of African #time# experience often desired in ethnographic accounts, these and other ethnographies of southern and eastern African peoples which treat the subject at all point out the tacit, practical, ad hoc character of #time#/"time" in this part of the world. Our Sesotho collocations attest copiously to these ethnographic observations.

COLLOCATIONAL EXPRESSION OF TIME IN SESOTHO

Ethnographic accounts seem nearly unanimous in reporting for southern and eastern Africa that #time# is a very immediate, existent, concrete reality. #Time# would seem to share this phenomenal reality with most of the rest of the lived world, upon which Bantu-speaking peoples bestow an apodictic "there-ness."

If one asks in a Bantu language, "How are you," one often hears in reply, "I'm here" (*ke fano*) or "I'm there" (*ke teng*). These replies are not sarcastic, ironic, or perfunctory. They mean in paraphrase: I am suitably, appropriately, felicitously present or situated; I'm O.K.

The various senses of the deictic, "there" in English, comprise meanings that express a variable weighting of abstract existence and of sensate presence. "There" in the following sentences seems to exhibit a decreasingly locative and an increasingly existential significance:

There are the cattle, in the field over there.
There are cattle in the field.
There are cattle to be put into the field.
There's nothing but rocks in the field.
There *is* no field.
There's nothing to be said the about the field.
There's no such thing as rock-eating cattle.

In Bantu languages, the existential deictics, including the counterpart to "there," do not so easily let go of their here-and-nowness. Existence is presence, not simply abstract being. For Bantu-speaking peoples the negation of *being* would seem to be *no-thingness-there*. Concordantly, reality is very sensate, very concretely material in a philosophic sense. So what can't be experienced isn't real. Interestingly, notions and senses of "time" are part and parcel of this *Weltanschauung*. These ideas are given all kinds of linguistic expression.

I myself was quite surprised by the numerousness of collocations that predicate of time a material existence: time is a partible entity, its effects, and a medium in motion. Even more to the point, specific expressions show time to be experienced as a very immediate, sensate construction, like space. For example, the causative mode of the verb collocates with time (*nako*) as its logical subject and signifies that the subject is ergodic—it brings about what the simple stem of the verb signifies. Causative verbs require of their subjects that they be capable of causing. In list B, time is its effects, we see many such causative expressions:

nako e ea hlahisa	(causes events)
apola	(discloses, reveals
honyolla	(extirpates)
upolla	(unearths)
utolla	(uproots)
rarolla	(untangles)
fenya	(conquers)

In Bantu languages the passive voice is used, unlike the case in English, when one wishes to stress the role of agency played by the logical subject. This role of agency is freely predicated of time. For example, from list B, we see:

khakhathiloe ke linako (to be thrashed repeatedly by time; *linako* = *nako*)
ruthuthiloe ke linako (to be wrestled by time)

from list E:

lahleheloa ke nako (to be lost by time)
fetoa ke nako (to be passed by time)

In Bantu languages there is a morphologically marked distinction between the identificative and the descriptive copulative. That is, if one wishes to express simple category inclusion or identity, like "the lion is an animal," one form of the copulative is used. If one wishes to use a category attributively or descriptively, as in "the lion is fierce," to predicate some quality, characteristic, or condition of the subject, one uses another verb form. Time (*nako*), like almost any material object, freely collocates both with predicates that identify it or include it in other categories and with predicates that attribute qualities to it. For example, from list B we note:

nako (time) *ke* (identificative "is")	*ntat'a tsohle* (the father of all)
	mookameli (one who dominates)
	sesinyi (a destroyer)
	sebalatsatsi (leveler)
	leruo (cattle, wealth)
nako (time) Ø (descriptive "is")	*mohale oa bahale* (the bravest) from list C
nako (time) *e* (descriptive "is")	*gaufi* (near) from list D
nako (time) *e* (descriptive "is")	*khut'soane* (short)

Time's materiality is expressed in those collocations that place time in the object position of sentences to be acted upon by causative verbs. From list E:

lekanya nako	(heft, weigh, compare—i.e., "estimate" time)
fetisa nako	(pass time)

The collocations for time as a course impute to time much more physical detail than we have found in collocations from the other languages:

nako e kana	(time of this spatial length)
hloelisa nako tse tlang	(to look from above at time coming)
ile boilatsatsi	(gone to the place of no time)
go tsamaea le linako	(to accompany time on foot)
mehlaleng ea nako	(paths of time)
maqhubung a nako	(in the waves/wanderings of time)
nako ea noaboloha	(time meanders lethargically)

These Sesotho collocations amply express culturally particular experiences of #time#, which have been reported ethnographically—a few of which have been indicated here. But, more important for our purposes, they provide us with very convincing evidence against the claim that "time" collocations and similarities among them might be explained by the *longue durée* accumulation of philosophic thought concerning #time#: the Sotho do not have such thought and never have had. Yet, as we see, they have and use collocations every bit as numerous and having the same categorial structure as those in English, Mandarin, and Hindi. Moreover, many of the particular metaphors that occur within specific categories, whether English, Mandarin, or Hindi, also appear in Sesotho.

To be sure, there aren't many collocations that predicate an orbital quality or a course to time. There are few, if any, collocations that bespeak the metrication of time. On the other hand, space-time deixis in Sesotho is identical to that in English and Hindi and recognizably similar to that in Mandarin. There is a key term, *nako*, which shows very wide and very similar privileges of collocation within and between categories as that shown by the counterpart terms—"time" in English, "*shi*" in Mandarin, and "*samay/waqt*" in Hindi/Urdu.

If we accept, as I argue we must, that collocation reflects language usage, including the ideological background and institutionalization of speaking, then clearly the Sotho talk about time in much the way English, Mandarin, and Hindi speakers do. Now our ethnographic accounts suggest that specific beliefs concerning time are not systematically organized among the Sotho. If this is so, what induces or structures dialogue and discourse about #time# among the Basotho so as to create this convergence of collocation and metaphoric categorization with very different cultures in Europe and Asia?

In my view, there is but one answer to this question, which has been the central point of this exercise: in large measure the experience of #time# is constituted by the embodied, enculturated mind as such and appears in language use or language patterning as a universal stock of collocations. Clearly, the Sesotho collocations didn't trickle down from great texts, oral or written, philosophic exegeses of itinerant sages. They were, as the Veda says, "cooked" from ordinary experience in daily life. We cannot, in my view, show any straightforward connection between a systematic cosmology (one doesn't really exist) and the categorial structure of Sesotho time collocations.

Ethnographic descriptions of time apperception among most Bantu-speaking people have to be carefully elicited—even goaded—from respondents or supplied by the interpreter. These descriptions are not ones native speakers articulate on their own, the way they do a folk tale, myth, or legend. This is quite opposed to the philosophically informed folk wisdom about "time" found in Europe, China, or India, which one can hear or overhear in many conversations.

The hypothesis of a panspecific, experiential *Bauplan* argues that the connection at some level between language (i.e., collocation) and culture will be one to many—a "homomorphism." The many Sesotho time collocations express something like a *default value* of #time# experience, which requires, of course, some cultural context for its appearance. But these collocations do *not* require overt ideological elaboration as such for them to appear in the language as expressions of experience. This experience is caused, I submit, by properties of being human, living in human communities, under *any* system of cultural sociality. There would be no point in linking—nor any way that we could link—the Sesotho time collocations to overt ideological, institutional, or ecological characteristics.

This lack of explicit connection leads us to two conclusions. First, even in the absence of systematic ideologies of #time# within a given culture, numerous collocations of time will be in use and will express an "innate" experience of #time#, with a distinct, universal category structure. Second, taken together, data from the four languages/cultures examined here show that culturally specific ideologies and institutional arrangements bearing on the experience of #time# preserve the basic categorial structure of "time," even while augmenting, suppressing, or extending its metaphoric content.

CHAPTER SEVEN

Conclusions

There is an important possible objection to the conclusions drawn on the strength of the Sesotho data. A number of scholars (Fabian 1983; Ong 1982; Thornton 1980; Tyler 1987) have argued that the Western cultural milieu imbues social science with an ideological bias peculiar to the West. Tyler calls this the "hegemony of the visual"; Fabian calls it "visualism"—"that ideological bias toward vision as the 'noblest sense' and toward geometry *qua* graphic-spatial conceptualization as the most exact way of communicating knowledge" (Fabian 1983:106). Although the roots of this bias go back a long way in time, Fabian notes—correctly, I think—that the social sciences inherited the intellectual formulation of this ideology from Descartes's delight with the visual as an exemplification of the mental (*res cogitans/res extensa*) and Hobbes's fascination with geometry.

One consequence of the "hegemony of the visual," according to Tyler (1987:150), is that it "necessitates a reductive ontological correlation between the visual and the verbal," which imbues the rhetoric of social science with a "metaphysics of substance . . . a sophisticated version of our naive physicalism . . . derived from and sustained by the metaphysical hegemony of the visual" (1987:152). The visual/spatial root metaphor pervades both common sense and scientific discourse in the West. Ong argues (1982) that the beginnings and the early importance of writing in Western cultures objectified language and gave it a spatial, visual extension that restructured consciousness, changing its sensory emphasis from oral-aural to primarily visual-spatial. For Fabian, it is not just our homely, common-sense way of talking which elevates the visual; learned discourse indulges in it even more flagrantly (1983:156).

Are the data we have gathered from India, China, and Africa an artifact of such a pervasive ideological bias? Have collocations been torn from their proper context and then been cut, stretched, or bent to fit a Cartesian bed of Procrustes? The answer, for two good reasons, is no. First, the collocations were not invented or culled selectively from more numerous and nonspatialized metaphors of time. Indeed, this research painstakingly sought collocations of any conceivable sort which might in any way express an experience of time. What we have seen is everything that could be elicited within the confines of this methodology.

Second, the arguments of Fabian, Ong, Tyler, and others are, in my view, correct only insofar as they describe a conscious project in the West, beginning in the Enlightenment, to conceive of thought on analogy with geometry. This project, so far as I can see, drew upon a stock of common-sense knowledge that appears not very different in regard to spatial/visual bias from what is found linguistically sedimented and articulated in discourse of many, if not all, languages/cultures. Indeed, the collocational data presented here suggest that the experience of #crude space# is a powerful predicate in metaphors of "time" in each of the four cultures examined. This remains true, despite very different, culturally peculiar appropriations, augmentations, and reworking of these stock expressions/experiences in the formulation of cosmologic ideas. The collocations in Sesotho, a language of an "oral" tradition, do not stand out as different quantitatively or qualitatively from those in the other three languages, each of which has been part of a "written" tradition for millennia.

Because culture structures and patterns the conditions of language use, it is obvious that collocations will express culturally particular experience. What is not so obvious is that there are experiences to which any language spoken in any culture will give expression. These *necessary* experiences will subsist despite cultural differences that overlay, qualify, or augment them. We have discovered in #time# and "time" a genuine necessary universal.

This is instantiated by five striking features to be found in the collocational data. First, in each of the four languages there are many words with temporal significance. Yet there is in each language a key, single lexical item having wide privileges of collocation across the categories of metaphor which are predicated of time: (1) "time" in English, (2) "*shi*" in Mandarin, (3) "*samay*" or "*waqt*" in Hindi-Urdu, and (4) "*nako*" in Sesotho.

Second, in each language there are a large number of collocations in each of the five major categories (Hindi's seeming lack of time as a line or orbit excepted).

Third, in each of the languages, collocations seem to fall into five (natural?) kinds or types based on the fundamental metaphor that contains "time" in either its "source" domain or "target" co-domain: (1) a partible entity, (2) a causal force or effect, (3) a medium in motion, (4) a course, or (5) an artifact of ascertainment or measurement.

Fourth, within each metaphor-defined category of collocation, there are a large number of specific lexical items and lexical senses entering into metaphoric predication with the word for "time" common to all four languages. Examples within each of the five categories include:

1. Time: wasting, saving, having, using, filling, ripening
2. Time: destroying, wearing, revealing, healing, befalling, happening, making happen
3. Time: flowing, moving, passing, coming, waiting, fleeting, bearing events with it, conducting events in it
4. Time (deixis) is: ahead, behind, in front, looked into/ back upon; time has: location, accompanies, comes round. More specifically, time can be a course without facing or direction through which the speaker moves or gazes, thereby imparting on it (time) the speaker's front (before), here/now, back (behind), then orientation. Or, conversely, time is a medium in motion, with its own forward (before) now, behind (after, afterward, then) orientation that imposes its facing and directionality onto the speaker or the events contained in the medium.

5. Time is: lost, kept, minded, discerned, marked, gained, divided, told

Fifth, the conscious philosophic elaboration of thought concerning the nature or experience of time in any culture seems to be confined to the selection and embellishment of one or more of the metaphoric categories that appear to be experiential universals. Thus the Greeks like the idea of time as a medium of motion in a circular orbit. The Romans (Christians) like the idea of time as a linear course with a beginning and end. The Chinese like the idea of time as a medium in motion bearing already scheduled events. The Indians like the idea of time as an all-encompassing entity without beginning, end, or even linearity filled with all kinds of powers and purposes. The Sotho have a two-dimensional apperception of time as a kind of space in which events take place—in and through which the individual moves. Even modern scientific treatments of relativistic time (e.g., "time" as one dimension of a four-dimensional space-time manifold) trade heavily on those universal categories and metaphors of time experience we have described above.

These data suggest the need to rethink the distinction made famous by Durkheim (1947), by Durkheim and Mauss (1963), and by Gurvitch (1964), and elaborated by such writers as Whorf, Leach, Geertz, Hall, and many other "relativists," that the experience and expression of time is based solely on the character of ideologies and social institutions—the rhythms of social life. Specifically, we should question, or at least severely qualify, their assertion that there is a categorial difference between conceptions of time in static, closed, cold, primitive societies versus those in dynamic, open, modern ones. While there is no doubt that differences do exist among cultures, these differences seem circumscribed and based on universally shared, everyday experience. Further, if experience as "subjective" as that of #time# can exhibit such commonality and hence intersubjectivity across distinct and unrelated (or remotely related) languages and markedly different cultures, it seems highly likely we humans share other notions, concepts, and experiences that arise from embodied, enculturated cognition.

More generally, I believe this study of #time# and "time" has substantiated Merleau-Ponty's claim that "to have a body is to possess a universal setting, a schema of all types of perceptual unfolding and of all those inter-sensory correspondences which lie beyond the segment of the world which we are actually perceiving. A thing is therefore not actually given in perception; it is internally taken up by us, reconstituted and experienced . . . in so far as it is bound up with a world, the basic structures of which we carry with us" (1962:326). "In language . . . man superimposes on the given world the world according to man" (Merleau-Ponty 1962:188).

Still, the "world according to man" is only empirically experienced by particular women and men in particular times and places, in terms of particular institutions, ideologies, intentions, and purposes. Although the collocations we have examined inhabit different parts of the globe and of history and are derived and constructed, in some cases, of culturally contingent belief and knowledge, we recognize all of them as familiar.

These conclusions bear importantly on the problem raised by W.V.O. Quine: the "impossibility of radical translation" (1960:26–57). Quine argues—correctly—that no amount of examination of what a sentence refers to or the subject that it is about is sufficient to constitute or reveal its meaning. Therefore, if people do not share a language in common, they can never be able to know or prove by virtue of experience that what a sentence or discourse means or might refer to in one language is equivalent to what they might mean or refer to in another. The world and our "direct" reference to it, says Quine, cannot serve as an independent measure of what sentences mean. Since reference always underdetermines meaning, we cannot be sure of what another is talking about unless we share a language and a culture to begin with.

Our study suggests what is wrong with Quine's problem, "the impossibility of radical translation": in a fundamental way, languages—and therefore cultures—cannot be *radically* different—that is, different at the *roots*. We have adduced evidence in the case of "time" that all languages/cultures are *rooted* in a panhuman experience. So, if all languages/cultures share and express a universal—that is, species-specific—ontology, translation among them is necessarily never "radical" at all. While cultural particularity is necessary to the existence and the expression of this fundament of shared experience, these particularities cannot alone be constitutive of its universality.

We have argued and sought to demonstrate, at least in the case of "time," that semantic meaning is the expression of experience. To be this, the semantic component of language must be generative. The modal, syncategorematic typification of one experience (time) by another (a course, a medium in motion, a partible entity, a physical effect, a measurement) creates new experience that can in turn be changed again in subsequent typification. Categorially novel predication can take place, of course, among indefinitely many particular experiences. Our "time" collocations showed that such particulars as commodity production, mechanical calibration, travel or locomotion, the sensate properties of rivers, and so on can modally typify time in different ways and to different degrees, depending on the culture.

This process of typification appears to be open and continuous, since virtually *any* experience can become, by means of language, a signifier that can then typify another experience, either conventionally or metaphorically. Language not only expresses previous, conventionalized experience; it can take up experience previously sedimented and typify it in conventionally and in *categorially* new ways.

This *generative process,* called metaphor, can work across linguistic boundaries (as well as within a single language) because conventionally sedimented experience expressed in some exotic language and culture is available for typification in our language in precisely the same way as any novel, categorially new experience is available for subsequent conventional or novel typification. This continuous conventional and categorially novel typification is a basic semantic principle of language.

In Chapter 4 we showed that category-breaking syncategorematic predication (metaphor) creates an *interaction* of predicates and arguments in syntactic structures. This does not mean that the argument of a proposition is a thing or a fixed concept, nor is the predicate a definite description or a category in which the argument is placed. Rather, as showed iteratively in the example "time is the best teacher," both "time" and "best teacher" become glosses for indefinitely many intentional experiences that are evaluated as a product function of one another. The very same process underlies the metaphors of time. The source domains—entity, effect, course, medium in motion, and method of ascertainment—are open-ended sets of indefinitely many experiences that are experimentally mapped onto what in this case is the inchoate co-domain of "time." This process of metaphor over time yields collocations and new senses of lexical morphemes, which take on an unproblematic, taken-for-granted "literalness." So, in collocation, "time" comes to have quite naturally, unproblematically, and inherently the experiential properties of a spatial template.

Despite the semantic freedom granted by metaphor and collocation, the evidence presented here shows that people do not "choose" their metaphors willy-nilly. There seems to be a panspecific proclivity to conceive and think about #time# in terms of #space#. Still, we are not prisoners of particular metaphors or collocations. We can augment, change, even deny these, all with language that commends in this case a spatialized conception of time to us in the first place. Metaphor enables us to break out of the stock of received, at-hand, conventionally used types or categories, thereby creating new ones. These new categories or typifications seldom lose complete touch with the type destruction that engendered them. The lexicon and collocation record the process. Thus, what happens over time is available in time to the whole speech community. The weight of language and cultural history hangs on the words and collocations we choose.

In the smaller-scale studies and arguments presented in the first three chapters, I sought, in most general and abstract terms, to indicate the direction we should look in to answer the question, "What are the meanings conveyed in discourse understood to be *about*?" The answer is—has to be—*experience*. Now, experience (or, equivalently, consciousness of something) is always, as we have seen, *intentional*. Even brute "external" reality—that which might be transduced by our irritable receptors (eye, ear, touch)—significantly underdetermines perception, which in turn underdetermines experience. And, of course, acts of conscious intention themselves—thinking, imagining, devising, assuming, knowing, believing, realizing, trusting, judging, deciding, discerning, estimating, doubting, expecting, and so on—are experiences in no sense transduced, picked up, or even necessarily prompted from the environment.

All reality *for us* is posed in terms of just such intentional acts of consciousness. Although "things themselves," including possibly **time**, may exist in their own right, language cannot directly mime or report them. Our glimpses, even of the brutely external, are always from behind the veil of other equally pressing realities: our species being, language, and culture. For this reason alone, a *reduction* of temporal experience to some prepredicative "space-perception" and space-perception to sensation is not adequate, even if highly relevant, to an account of meaning invariance. This conclusion endorses, of course, a "cognitivist" view of perception (as argued by Fodor 1981) against an "ecological" or sensory one (as argued by Gibson 1979).

Translation—understanding across boundaries of particular languages, cultures, historical epochs, scientific paradigms, or literary texts—frequently and routinely requires novel typification, as well as textual elaboration above the level of the sentence. Such cross-language/culture/theory/genre understanding often cannot be obtained by appeal to familiar, conventional experience or expression. What is required, rather, is that same practice and interpretation invited by metaphor within a single language, cultural, or theoretic context.

Intersubjectivity across experiential chasms is possible because the semantic component of language includes a lexicon that is as open to new—even culturally novel—experience as are whole sentences. In this view, the lexicon is both a culture-historical repository and an open window on future possibility—the unshaped, material resource of the everyday wordsmith, the scientist, the artist.

While the Word was our collective beginning, the more we seek to articulate and communicate our particular experiences, the richer becomes our collective lexicon and our ability to share with others what we are in virtue of them.

REFERENCES

Abelson, Robert, and Robert Schank
 1977 *Scripts, Plans, and Understanding.* Hillsdale, N.J.: Erlbaum Associates.

Alverson, Hoyt
 1978 *Mind in the Heart of Darkness: Value and Self-identity among the Tswana of Southern Africa.* New Haven: Yale University Press.
 1984 "Phonology and the Foundations of Lévi-Strauss' Structuralism." *American Journal of Semiotics* 2, no. 4:99–123.
 1991 "Metaphor and Experience" in *Beyond Metaphor: The Theory of Tropes in Anthropology,* edited by J. W. Fernandez. Stanford: Stanford University Press.

Barwise, Jon, and John Perry
 1983 *Situations and Attitudes.* Cambridge: MIT Press.

Beidelman, T. O.
 1963 "Kaguru Time-Reckoning: An Aspect of Cosmology among an East African People." *Southwestern Journal of Anthropology* 19:9–20.

Berlin, Brent
 1968 *Tzeltal Numeral Classifiers.* The Hague: Mouton.

Berlin, Brent, Dennis E. Breedlove, and Peter H. Raven
 1974 *Principles of Tzeltal Plant Classification.* New York: Academic Press.

Berlin, Brent, and Paul Kay
 1969 *Basic Color Terms: Their Universality and Evolution.* Berkeley and Los Angeles: University of California Press.

Bettini, Maurizio
 1991 *Anthropology and Roman Culture: Kinship, Time, and Images of the Soul.* Baltimore: Johns Hopkins University Press.

Bickerton, Derek
 1990 *Language and Species.* Chicago: University of Chicago Press, 1990.

Black, Max
  1979 "More about Metaphor." In *Metaphor and Thought,* edited by Andrew Ortony. New York: Cambridge University Press.

Bolinger, Dwight
  1961 "Syntactic Blends and Other Matters." *Language* 37:366–81.
  1965 "The Atomization of Meaning." *Language* 41:555–73.
  1967 "Adjectives in English: Attribution and Predication." *Lingua* 10:1–34.
  1975 *Aspects of Language.* 2d ed. New York: Harcourt, Brace.
  1980 *Language: The Loaded Weapon.* London: Longman.

Bordieu, P.
  1963 "The Attitude of the Algerian Peasant toward Time." In *Mediterranean Countrymen,* edited by J. Pitt-Rivers. The Hague: Mouton.

Boyd, Richard
  1979 "Metaphor and Theory Change." In *Metaphor and Thought.* See Black 1979.

Brandon, S.G.F.
  1964 *History, Time, and Deity.* New York: Barnes and Noble.

Braudel, Fernand
  1984 *Civilization and Capitalism, Fifteenth to Eighteenth Centuries.* New York: Harper and Row.

Carnap, Rudolph
  1966 *Philosophical Foundations of Physics.* New York: Basic Books.

Casson, Ronald
  1981 *Language, Culture, and Cognition.* New York: Macmillan.

Clark, E. V.
  1971 "On the Acquisition of the Meaning of *Before* and *After.*" *Journal of Verbal Learning and Verbal Behavior* 10:266–75.
  1973 "How Children Describe Time and Order." In *Studies of Child Language Development,* edited by C. A. Ferguson and D. I. Slobin. New York: Holt, Rinehart, and Winston.

Clark, Herbert
  1973 "Space, Time, Semantics, and the Child." In *Cognitive Development and the Acquisition of Language,* edited by T. E. Moore. New York: Academic Press.

Durkheim, E.
  1947 *The Elementary Forms of Religious Life.* Glencoe, Ill.: Free Press.

Durkheim, E., and M. Mauss
1963 *Primitive Classification*. Chicago: University of Chicago Press.

Edie, James
1976 *Speaking and Meaning*. Evanston, Ill.: Northwestern University Press.
1987 *Edmund Husserl's Phenomenology: A Critical Commentary*. Bloomington: Indiana University Press.

Fabian, Johannes
1983 *Time and the Other: How Anthropology Makes Its Object*. New York: Columbia University Press.

Fernandez, James W., ed.
1991 *Beyond Metaphor: The Theory of Tropes in Anthropology*. Stanford: Stanford University Press.

Firth, J. R.
1957 *Papers in Linguistics, 1934–1951*. London: Oxford University Press.

Fodor, Janet
1980 *Semantics: Theories of Meaning in Generative Grammar*. Cambridge: Harvard University Press.

Fodor, Jerry
1981 "How Direct Is Visual Perception? Some Reflections on Gibson's 'Ecological Approach.'" *Cognition* 9 (April):139–96.
1983 *The Modularity of Mind: An Essay in Faculty Psychology*. Cambridge: MIT Press.

Frake, Charles
1985 "Cognitive Maps of Time and Tide among Medieval Seafarers." *Man: Journal of the Royal Anthropological Institute* 20:254–70.

Fraser, J. T.
1987 *Time: The Familiar Stranger*. Amherst: University of Massachusetts Press.

Frege, Gottlob
1974 "On Sense and Reference." In *Readings in Semantics*, edited by Farhang Zabeeh et al. Urbana: University of Illinois Press.

Geertz, Clifford
1973a "The Growth of Culture and the Evolution of Mind." In *The Interpretation of Cultures*. New York: Basic Books.
1973b "The Impact of the Concept of Culture on the Concept of Man." In *The Interpretation of Cultures*. See Geertz 1973a.

1973c "Person, Time, and Conduct in Bali." In *The Interpretation of Cultures*. See Geertz 1973a.

Gell, Alfred
1992 *The Anthropology of Time: Cultural Constructions of Temporal Maps and Images*. Oxford: Berg.

Gibson, J.
1979 *The Ecological Approach to Visual Perception*. Boston: Houghton Mifflin.

Givens, Douglas R.
1977 *An Analysis of Navajo Temporality*. Washington, D.C.: University Press of America.

Graesser, Arthur, and Leslie F. Clark
1985 *Structures and Procedures of Implicit Knowledge*. Norwood,N.J.: Ablex.

Gurevich, A. J. ed.
1976 *Cultures and Time*. Paris: UNESCO.

Gurvitch, Georges
1964 *The Spectrum of Social Time*. Dordrecht: Reidel.

Hall, Edward
1984 *The Dance of Life: The Other Dimension of Time*. New York: Anchor Books.

Hesse, Mary
1966 *Models and Analogies in Science*. Notre Dame, Ind.: University of Notre Dame Press.

Hobsbawm, E. J.
1984 *Workers: Worlds of Labor*. New York: Pantheon.

Holland, Dorothy
1987 *Cultural Models in Language and Thought*. New York: Cambridge University Press.

Horton, Robin
1970 "African Traditional Thought and Western Science." In *Rationality*, edited by Bryan Wilson. New York: Harper and Row.

Jackendoff, Ray
1983 *Semantics and Cognition*. Cambridge: MIT Press.

Jardine, Nick
1980 "The Possibility of Absolutism." In *Science, Belief, and Behavior*, edited by D. H. Mellor. Cambridge: Cambridge University Press.

Johnson, Mark
1987   *The Body in the Mind*. Chicago: University of Chicago Press.

Kant, Immanuel
1953   *Critique of Pure Reason*. Translated by Norman K. Smith. New York: Macmillan.

Katz, Jerrold J.
1972   *Semantic Theory*. New York: Harper and Row.
1979   "Semantics and Conceptual Change." *Philosophical Review* (July):327–65.

Katz, Jerrold J., and Jerry Fodor
1963   "The Structure of a Semantic Theory." *Language* 39:170–210.

Kay, Paul
1979   "The Role of Cognitive Schemata in Word Meaning: Hedges Revisited." Manuscript, Department of Linguistics, University of California, Berkeley.

Kay, Paul, and Willett Kempton
1983   "What Is the Sapir-Whorf Hypothesis?" Berkeley Cognitive Science Report 8, Berkeley Cognitive Science Program, University of California, Berkeley.

Kay, Paul, and Chad McDaniel
1978   "The Linguistic Significance of the Meanings of Basic Color Terms." *Language* 54:610–46.

Keesing, Roger M.
1991   "Time, Cosmology, and Experience." Manuscript, Department of Anthropology, McGill University, Montreal.

Kempton, Willett
1981   *Folk Classification of Ceramics: A Study of Cognitive Prototypes*. New York: Academic Press.

Lakoff, George
1987   *Women, Fire, and Dangerous Things*. Chicago: University of Chicago Press.

Lakoff, George, and Mark Johnson
1980   *Metaphors We Live By*. Chicago: University of Chicago Press.

Langacker, Ronald
1987   *Foundations of Cognitive Grammar*. Vol. 1, *Theoretical Prerequisites*. Stanford: Stanford University Press.
1988   "A View of Linguistic Semantics." In *Topics in Cognitive Linguistics*, edited by Brygida Rudzka-Ostyn. Amsterdam: John Benjamins.

1990   *Concept of Image and Symbol: The Cognitive Basis of Grammar.* Berlin: DeGruyter.

Lappin, Shalom
1981   *Sorts, Ontology, and Metaphor.* Berlin: DeGruyter.

Larre, Claude
1976   "The Empirical Apperception of Time and the Conception of History in Chinese Thought." in Gurevich 1976.

Leach, Edmund
1961   "Cronus and Chronos." In *Rethinking Anthropology.* London: Athlone Press.

Lévi-Strauss, Claude
1966   *The Savage Mind.* Chicago: University of Chicago Press.

Lightfoot, David
1987   *The Language Lottery: Toward a Biology of Grammars.* Cambridge: MIT Press.

Lloyd, G.E.R.
1976   "Views on Time in Greek Thought." In Gurevich 1976.

Lyons, John
1977   *Semantics* (Vol. 2). Cambridge: Cambridge University Press.
1989   "Semantic Ascent: A Neglected Aspect of Syntactic Typology." In *Essays on Grammatical Theory and Universal Grammar*, edited by Doug Arnold. Oxford: Clarendon Press.

MacCormac, Earl R.
1985   *A Cognitive Theory of Metaphor.* Cambridge: MIT Press.

Macey, Samuel L.
1980   *Clocks and the Cosmos: Time in Western Life and Thought.* Hamden, Conn.: Archon Books.

Mandal, K. K.
1968   *A Comparative Study of the Concepts of Space and Time in Indian Thought.* Varanas: Chowhamba Sanskrit Studies, Vol. LXV.

Margenau, Henry
1950   *The Nature of Physical Reality: A Philosophy of Modern Physics.* New York: McGraw-Hill.

McGinn, Colin
1981   "Modal Reality." In *Reduction, Time, and Reality*, edited by Richard Healey. London: Cambridge University Press.

Merleau-Ponty, Maurice
1962   *Phenomenology of Perception.* Translated by Colin Smith. London: Routledge and Kegan Paul.

Miller, George A., and P. N. Johnson-Laird
1976   *Language and Perception.* Cambridge: Harvard University Press.

Mitchell, T. F.
1971   "Linguistic Goings On. . . ." *Archivum Linguisticum,* n.s., 2:35–69.

Mohanty, James
1970   *Phenomenology and Ontology.* The Hague: Martinus Nijhof.

Munn, Nancy
1992   "The Cultural Anthropology of Time: A Critical Essay." *Annual Review of Anthropology* 21:93–123.

Nakamura, Hajime
1966   "Time in Indian and Japanese Thought." In *The Voices of Time,* edited by J. T. Fraser. New York: George Braziller.

Needham, Joseph
1965   *Time and Eastern Man.* The Henry Myers Lecture, 1964. London: Royal Anthropological Institute of Great Britain and Ireland.

Neher, Andre
1976   "The View of Time and History in Jewish Culture." In Gurevich 1976.

Newmeyer, Frederick J.
1980   *Linguistic Theory in America: The First Quarter-Century of Transformational Generative Grammar.* New York: Academic Press.
1986   *The Politics of Linguistics.* Chicago: University of Chicago Press.

Newmeyer, Frederick J., ed.
1988   *Linguistic Theory.* Vol. 1, *Foundations.* New York: Cambridge University Press.

Ong, Walter J.
1982   *Orality and Literacy: Technologizing the Word.* London: Methuen.

Ortiz, Alfonso
1969   *The Tewa World: Space, Time, Being, and Becoming in a Pueblo Society.* Chicago: University of Chicago Press.

Panikkar, Raimundo
1976   "Time and History in the Tradition of India. . . ." In Gurevich 1976.

Pattaro, Germano
1976   "The Christian Conception of Time." In Gurevich 1976.

Quine, W.V.O.
1960   *Word and Object.* Cambridge: MIT Press.

Ricoeur, Paul
1967   *Husserl: An Analysis of His Phenomenology*. Evanston, Ill.: Northwestern University Press.

Rosch, Eleanor
1973   "Natural Categories." *Cognitive Psychology* 4:328–50.
1975   "Cognitive Representations of Natural Categories." *Journal of Experimental Psychology* 104:192–233.
1977   "Human Categorization." In *Studies in Cross-cultural Psychology*, edited by N. Warren. New York: Academic Press.
1978   "Principles of Categorization." In *Cognition and Categorization*, edited by Eleanor Rosch and B. B. Lloyd. Hillsdale, N.J.: Erlbaum Associates.
1981   "Prototype Classification and Logical Classification: The Two Systems." In *New Trends in Cognitive Representation: Challenges to Piaget's Theory*, edited by E. Scholnik. Hillsdale, N.J.: Erlbaum Associates.

Rudzka-Ostyn, Brygida
1988   *Topics in Cognitive Linguistics*. Philadelphia: J. Benjamins.

Russell, Bertrand
1905   "On Denoting." In *Readings in Semantics*. See Frege 1974.

Talmy, Leonard
1975   "Semantics and Syntax of Motion." In *Syntax and Semantics*, vol. 4, edited by John P. Kimball. New York: Academic Press.
1978   "Figure and Ground in Complex Sentences." In *Universals of Human Language*. Vol. 4, *Syntax*, edited by Joseph Greenberg et al. Stanford: Stanford University Press.
1983   "How Language Structures Space." Berkeley Cognitive Science Report, Berkeley Cognitive Science Program, University of California, Berkeley.
1985   "Lexicalization Patterns: Semantic Structure in Lexical Forms." In *Language Typology and Syntactic Descriptions*. Vol. 3, *Grammatical Categories and the Lexicon*, edited by Timothy Shopen. London: Cambridge University Press.

Tannen, Deborah
1989   *Talking Voices: Repetition, Dialogue, and Imagery in Conversational Discourse*. Cambridge: Cambridge University Press.

Thornton, Robert J.
1980   *Space, Time, and Culture among the Iraqw of Tanzania*. New York: Academic Press.

Traugott, Elizabeth Closs
1975 "Spatial Expressions of Tense and Temporal Sequencing: A Contribution to the Study of Semantic Fields." *Semiotica* 15:207–30.
1978 "On the Expression of Spatio-Temporal Relations in Language." In *Universals of Human Language*. Vol. 3, *Word Structure*. See Talmy 1978.

Tyler, Stephen A.
1978 *The Said and the Unsaid: Mind, Meaning, and Culture*. New York: Academic Press.
1987 *The Unspeakable: Discourse, Dialogue, and Rhetoric in the Postmodern World*. Madison: University of Wisconsin Press.

Tyler, Stephen A., ed.
1987 *Cognitive Anthropology: Readings*. Prospect Heights, Ill.: Waveland Press.

Weyl, Hermann
1970 "On Space, Time, and Matter." In *Phenomenology and the Natural Sciences*, edited by Joseph Kockelmans and Theodore Kisiel. Evanston, Ill.: Northwestern University Press.

Whorf, Benjamin Lee
1940 "Science and Linguistics." *Technology Review* 44:229–47.
1956 *Language, Thought, and Reality: Selected Writings*. Edited and with an introduction by John B. Carroll. Cambridge: MIT Press.

Wierzbicka, Anna
1992 *Semantics, Culture, and Cognition: Universal Human Concepts in Culture-Specific Configurations*. New York: Oxford University Press.

Witherspoon, Gary
1977 *Language and Art in the Navajo Universe*. Ann Arbor: University of Michigan Press.

Worsley, Peter
1984 *The Three Worlds: Culture and Development*. Chicago: University of Chicago Press.

Zwart, P. J.
1976 *About Time*. Amsterdam: North Holland.

INDEX

Library of Congress Cataloging-in-Publication Data

Alverson, Hoyt, 1942–
   Semantics and experience : universal metaphors of time in English,
   Mandarin, Hindi, and Sesotho / Hoyt Alverson.
        P.   cm. — (Parallax)
   Includes bibliographical references and index.
   ISBN 0-8018-4811-3 (acid-free paper)
   1. Space and time in language.   2. Semantics.   3. Language and
   culture.   4. Metaphor.   I. Title.   II. Series: Parallax
   (Baltimore, Md.)
   P37.5.S65A47   1994
   401'.43—dc20   93-40748